Spring 1996   Vol. XVI, no. 1
ISSN: 0276-0045   ISBN: 1-56478-395-2

THE REVIEW OF CONTEMPORARY FICTION

Editor
JOHN O'BRIEN
Illinois State University

Senior Editor
ROBERT L. MCLAUGHLIN
Illinois State University

Associate Editor
IRVING MALIN

Guest Editor
DAVID FOSTER WALLACE

Typesetter
SHIRLEY GEEVER

Production & Design
N. J. FURL

Editorial Assistants
RICHARD BLANKENSHIP
REBECCA COOPER

Cover Art
YOKO KAWAZOE

The *Review of Contemporary Fiction* is published three times a year (January, June, September) by the Center for Book Culture at Illinois State University (ISU Campus Box 8905, Normal, IL 61790-8905). ISSN 0276-0045. Subscription prices are as follows:

Single volume (three issues):
  Individuals: $17.00; foreign, add $3.50;
  Institutions: $26.00; foreign, add $3.50.

DISTRIBUTION. Bookstores should send orders to:

Review of Contemporary Fiction, ISU Campus Box 8905,
Normal, IL 61790-8905. Phone 309-438-7555; fax 309-438-7422.

This issue is partially supported by a grant from the Illinois Arts Council, a state agency.

Indexed in *American Humanities Index, International Bibliography of Periodical Literature, International Bibliography of Book Reviews, MLA Bibliography,* and *Book Review Index.* Abstracted in *Abstracts of English Studies.*

The *Review of Contemporary Fiction* is also available on 16mm microfilm, 35mm microfilm, and 105mm microfiche from University Microfilms International, 300 North Zeeb Road, Ann Arbor, MI 48106-1346.

www.centerforbookculture.org

THE REVIEW OF CONTEMPORARY FICTION

BACK ISSUES AVAILABLE

Back issues are still available for the following numbers of the *Review of Contemporary Fiction* ($8 each unless otherwise noted):

NOVELIST AS CRITIC: Essays by Garrett, Barth, Sorrentino, Wallace, Ollier, Brooke-Rose, Creeley, Mathews, Kelly, Abbott, West, McCourt, McGonigle, and McCarthy

NEW FINNISH FICTION: Fiction by Eskelinen, Jäntti, Kontio, Krohn, Paltto, Sairanen, Selo, Siekkinen, Sund, Valkeapää

NEW ITALIAN FICTION: Interviews and fiction by Malerba, Tabucchi, Zanotto, Ferrucci, Busi, Corti, Rasy, Cherchi, Balduino, Ceresa, Capriolo, Carrera, Valesio, and Gramigna

GROVE PRESS NUMBER: Contributions by Allen, Beckett, Corso, Ferlinghetti, Jordan, McClure, Rechy, Rosset, Selby, Sorrentino, and others

NEW DANISH FICTION: Fiction by Brøgger, Høeg, Andersen, Grøndahl, Holst, Jensen, Thorup, Michael, Sibast, Ryum, Lynggaard, Grønfeldt, Willumsen, and Holm

NEW LATVIAN FICTION: Fiction by Nora Ikstena, Paul Bankovskis, Guntis Berelis, Arvis Kolmanis, Andra Neiburga, Rimants Ziedonis, and others

THE FUTURE OF FICTION: Essays by Birkerts, Caponegro, Franzen, Galloway, Maso, Morrow, Vollmann, White, and others ($15)

NEW JAPANESE FICTION: Interviews and fiction by Ohara, Shimada, Shono, Takahashi, Tsutsui, McCaffery, Gregory, Kotani, Tatsumi, Koshikawa, and others

Individuals receive a 10% discount on orders of one issue and a 20% discount on orders of two or more issues. To place an order, use the form on the last page of this issue.

RCF Call for Contributors

www.centerforbookculture.org/review

The *Review of Contemporary Fiction* is seeking contributors to write overview essays on the following writers:

Felipe Alfau, Chandler Brossard, Gabrielle Burton, Michel Butor, Julieta Campos, Jerome Charyn, Emily Holmes Coleman, Stanley Crawford, Eva Figes, Karen Elizabeth Gordon, Carol De Chellis Hill, Violette Leduc, Olive Moore, Julián Ríos, Esther Tusquets.

The essays must:

- be fifty double-spaced pages;
- cover the subject's biography;
- summarize the critical reception of the subject's works;
- discuss the course of the subject's career, including each major work;
- provide interpretive strategies for new readers to apply to the subject's work;
- provide a bibliographic checklist of each of the subject's works (initial and latest printings);
- be written for a general, intelligent reader, who does not know the subject's work;
- avoid jargon, theoretical digressions, and excessive endnotes;
- be intelligent, interesting, and readable;
- be documented in MLA style.

Authors will be paid $250.00 when the essay is published. All essays will be subject to editorial review, and the editors reserve the right to request revisions and to reject unacceptable essays.

Applicants should send a CV and a brief writing sample. In your cover letter, be sure to address your qualifications.

Send applications to:

Robert L. McLaughlin
Dalkey Archive Press, Illinois State University, Campus Box 8905, Normal, IL 61790-8905

Inquiries: rmclaugh@ilstu.edu

Contents

_____

Focus on Mexico

_____

Quo Vadis—Introduction

David Foster Wallace

HI. I'VE NEVER REALLY edited anything before, but I'm the one who's edited this "Quo Vadis" number of *RCF*. This job involved sending out a letter about a year and a half ago inviting a number of writers and editors under c. forty-five to write whatever they wanted on the topic of where they thought literary art* was heading in the next century. I'll spare you a reproduction of this letter. Plus the job involved interfacing with the Dalkey Archive Press people about whom to invite to contribute, and then reinterfacing with them when some of the original people on the list said no or said yes and then bailed out and then other people who hadn't been on the list heard about the list and thought maybe they'd like to write a Quo-Vadisish essay and were added to the list. The final list is about 50 percent Dalkey and 50 percent me. Then the job involved reading the essays as they came in and copyediting them—I'm a good copy editor, and this has been the only really comfortable part of the whole process as far as I'm concerned.

So here are twelve essays. If you flip one page back you can see for yourself who they're by. I won't try to sum up any of the essays or do some discursive thing about what the overall gist of the collective seems to be— the pieces themselves are mostly pretty discursive, and I don't feel like anybody wants to hear me discursing about discursion. In a way, the essays already summarize themselves pretty well. Some of them are really dark. More than a few are pissed off about various things. Some of the essays are funny, and a couple have really pretty prose. Some take an attitude toward contemporary culture and government that I think is self-pitying and beetle-spirited. A couple of the essays are kind of inspiring. I find about three-quarters of them interesting, finally.

I have observed in myself a kind of sine-wavelike cycle of interest and boredom and interest in riding herd on a project like this. In a way it's sort of like my cycle of feelings about religion. To me, religion is incredibly fascinating as a general abstract object of thought—it might be the most interesting thing there is. But when it gets to the point of trying to communicate specific or persuasive stuff about religion, I find I always get frustrated and bored. I think this is because the stuff that's truly interesting

---

*(literary art in general, or literary art in relation to culture, or all of these, or none)

about religion is inarticulable.** Plus the truth is that there's nothing about it I really *know*, and nothing about it that anybody, I don't think, really *knows;* and so when I hear some person try to articulate or persuade me of some specific point about religious stuff I find myself looking at my watch or shifting my feet, immediately and deeply bored. But—each time—this boredom always lasts exactly as long as it takes me to realize that what this person who's trying to talk about religion is really talking about is herself. This happens each time. I'm glazed and scanning for the exit until I get the real gist: though these heartfelt utterances present themselves as assuasive or argumentative, what they really are are—truly, deeply—*expressive*—expressive of a self's heart's special tangle, of a knowing and verbal self's particular tortured relation to what is unknow- and -sayable. Then it gets interesting again.

I know that each of the contributors to this number of *RCF* has a deep-felt stake in literary art and its future. I also know that not one of them is "right" in any argumentative or predictive sense.*** Nobody knows where anything important is going, really. And the deeper the stake a writer has in something, I think, the less reliable a diagnostician or forecaster she's going to be. But I think this is OK. I myself ended up reading these essays more like diary entries than anything else—the only real object of revelation is the writers themselves. I suppose this is S.O.P. for all essays, in a way.

**(Which of course paradoxically is a big part of what makes it so interesting, so it all gets really tangled.)

***(I think Jon Franzen's very, very close to being right, but this is because he and I are friends, and sort of rivals, and we argue about all this stuff, and from the way I read his piece here it seems to me that I've won and convinced him I'm right, so in general I'm just real pleased with Jon's essay.)

Second Thoughts

Sven Birkerts

A FEW YEARS AGO I wrote a series of essays in which I proclaimed that the enterprise of fiction was in a state of serious crisis—a state that had a number of causes but that was most obviously connected to our sudden submergence under the fast-breaking wave of electronic technologies. I premised these saturnine essays on a fairly basic assumption, one to which I still subscribe, namely: that the health of the novel ultimately depends on its ability to mirror and explore the culture of the present, and that if novelists find themselves unequal to the task of taking our mutating circumstances as subject matter, the genre will forfeit its deeper authority. I cited the inordinate difficulty of presenting our mediated experience in dramatic ways and listed what I saw as some of the strategies writers used to evade the challenge at hand. These included writing about the narrowly domestic; using conveniently unmediated small-town settings; and turning to the past, either historical or familial. Needless to say, my views did not please everyone. More than one novelist took me to task, some for the narrowness of my premise, others for what they perceived as my scorn for the subsidiary options.

I still hold to my core notion—that if the novel cannot digest the stuff of the present it will, in time, doom itself to irrelevance and lose whatever prophetic vitality it may yet possess as its modernist inheritance. But as I have continued to think about the coming of the electronic millennium—and continued to read novels of all descriptions—I have come to see that I need to make certain adjustments to my theory. To put it most simply: I had not fully thought through all of the implications of the cultural changes that are upon us. I had not thought enough about how these changes impinge upon our experience of time and history, and, in consequence, create a whole new category of need—one which the novel is wonderfully suited to meet.

So, without changing my original premise, I would add a second: that the time of the novel, the phenomenological interior which necessarily reorganizes the reader's perceptions, may just be the ideal antidote for the time-sickness that we are all, most of us unwittingly, beginning to experience. That the novel is not only a lens upon the present but also can serve to counteract some of the most pernicious tendencies of that present.

Postmodern time is, as we all know, fragmented, composed of competing simultaneities. Our daily operations pull us ineluctably away from the deep durational time experience that is, or was, our birthright. The novel, through language, through the complex decelerating system of syntax, pushes us against the momentum of distraction. It is restorative—and difficult. Indeed, it is often restorative precisely to the degree that it is difficult, especially as the difficulties of reading generally have as much to do with the reader's failures of attention as they do with the text on the page. One does not dive from CNN or *Masterpiece Theatre* into the deep brine of prose easily. All of the cognitive rhythms have to be slowed to andante.

I would argue, then, that the contemporary novelist who is not in any way addressing the changed reality of the present may yet be serving an important function. *For the reader,* that is—not necessarily for the genre itself. A crucial distinction. Through his deployment of the language, through giving expression to his vision, the writer may be creating a self-contained alternate order—a place where the ambitious reader can go to counter the centrifuge of late modernity, where he can, at least for a time, possess the aesthetic illusion of focus and sustain a single-minded immersion in circumstance no longer so generally available. That this is vicarious does not undermine its validity: it is a mode of surrogate living which most closely approximates what living felt like before technologies began to divide us from ourselves.

Any good novel, then (I won't quibble here about what constitutes "good"), can afford its reader a way of being—if not being *there,* in the other world, then being *here,* in this. It proposes a locus of reclamation, becomes a place inside the place we are situated, a charged time contained within the more diffuse time of daily living. And while this is not exactly a revolutionary function for the embattled genre, it will become increasingly important as the equation of existence grows complex beyond all calculation.

But this is general. The notion first came to me in far more specific terms, the product of one of those happy convergences that signals to me that I need to pay attention. One vector was my recent rereading of Richard Powers's novel, *Prisoner's Dilemma,* for a course I was teaching. The other was my near simultaneous encounter with Bradford Morrow's *Trinity Fields,* a novel I grabbed to read for pleasure during a family vacation. Here, I found, were two very different works which nonetheless shared something kindred at the core. *Prisoner's Dilemma* tells the story of Edward Hobson, a brilliant and idealistic man who succumbs to a strange illness and with the help of his wife and grown children creates a highly elastic web of denial around himself. Only the intensification of the illness itself can rupture the complicity of the family members. At this point getting to the root of the problem means diagnosing the life of the man himself, a process which soon enough means taking an exacting look at the larger movements of history in his life. Private circumstance is seen to be ultimately inextricable from the envelope of societal circumstance. All things are, in the manner of Chaos science, linked. And in this case the trail leads finally back to Alamogordo, New Mexico, the desert site of the A-bomb test. Everything that has happened to Edward Hobson and his family can be seen as part of the concentric system of effects originated at ground zero.

Morrow's *Trinity Fields,* by contrast, tells the decades-long story of two friends. Brice McCarthy and Kip Calder are both sons of research physicists working at Los Alamos. Born on the same day in 1944, they come of age in the 1950s and then again through the turmoils of the sixties. Both are shaped in complex and destructive ways by their deepening awareness of what their fathers—and their government—were responsible for. And, as in *Prisoner's Dilemma,* the consequences of a specific historical moment (the Trinity blast figured in the title) are played out over an extended period in what becomes a searching inquiry into the mechanism of moral consciousness.

The two novels were present in my thoughts, were already nearing some sort of catalysis, when I chanced to read the opening chapter of Harold Bloom's *The Western Canon* and encountered this assertion:

The historical novel seems to have been permanently devalued. Gore Vidal once said to me, with bitter eloquence, that his outspoken sexual orientation had denied him canonical status. What seems likelier is that Vidal's best fictions . . . are distinguished historical novels—*Lincoln, Burr,* and several more—and this subgenre is no longer available for canonization.

Here were the words to set off sparks in the contrarian's heart. Though I had, before, likewise relegated the historical novel to the cultural seconds bin—viewing it essentially as a detour around the subject matter crisis—now, in the wake of my reading of Powers and Morrow, I thought I understood a new possibility for the novel. And, as a result, I have had to revise my somewhat dogmatic premise of what it is that a novel can, and ought to, do.

Formerly I insisted that the true life—the raison d'être—of the genre lay in its comprehension and dramatization of our historical moment, our present. The novel was to be a kind of petri dish in which the novelist would explore the ever-changing terms of "how it is." This was the sovereign artistic task. The emphasis was placed squarely on the NOW, and all other initiatives were necessarily secondary.

I was, I admit, too stringent. My analysis of the novelist's function did not fully accord with my analysis of the new reality, the electronic millennium. I mean: Our mediated lives, our frenzied rush to get on-line, to build a web of impulses around ourselves, have not only led to a loss of subjective deep time but have also severed us from any comprehensive narrative of history—our own, but that of preceding epochs as well. We have stepped into the postmodern swirl of dissociated images and decontextualized data. We are overwhelmed with impressions and bits and are ever more at a loss to integrate the jumble we harvest into any coherent picture. If this is so—

and I write this in the days right after the Oklahoma City bomb blast, in the midst of the cataract of clips and chunks of horrifying data—then we are in dire need not only of works that reflect our present situation to us but also of works that process the things we may not have had the time or focus or will to deal with; works that serve as a kind of fertile unconscious out of which can be distilled the patterns and meanings we cannot live without. We need the novel, then, not only as a windshield through which to face what is in front of us but also as a rearview mirror that allows us to see where we have been. We need the form of the novel—the wrought artifact—because it makes available the kind of time essential for processing impressions and emotions. And we need specific works of historical imagination through which we can repossess what the exigencies of living in a high-speed information age are denying us. Seen in this way, the novel is a kind of slow-motion replay of materials that we have not been able to absorb properly. Unlike television sports, though, history comes into being only in retrospect. An event is not history—the etymological root of the word is *storia,* meaning *story* or *tale*—until it enters narrative. The narratives supplied to us by CNN and the daily press, premised on sensation and the kind of focus that magnifies and decontextualizes, are not vehicle enough. Nor can film, ideal though it is for visual simulation, offer the time immersion required. Nor can histories of the standard sort enlist the empathic imagination essential for true narrative engagement. It falls to the novel. And as we hasten away from centers and certainties, as the brave new world wraps us up in its oscillating energy field, the sense-making powers of the novel are one of our most valuable resources. If only we can buck the momentum of the present enough to recognize this; then buck it further to act upon our recognition.

Crackpot Realism: Fiction for the Forthcoming Millennium

Melvin Jules Bukiet

> A man must be a little mad if he does not want to be even more stupid.
>
> —Montaigne

THERE ARE TWO KINDS of literature that endure: that which utterly transcends its era, and that which perfectly reflects it. Most writers of contemporary fiction wish to inhabit the first realm. They ponder questions of love, loneliness, and death. More eloquently or less eloquently, their voices range from the most traditionally centered writers to only recently enfranchised multiculturalists, from John Updike to David Leavitt or Gloria Naylor. No matter their differences, all of them are conservative—in a literary rather than political sense. They tell the kinds of stories we have heard before. The shapes of these stories are familiar, even if their characters are new. These writers are fundamentally ahistoric.

From the *New Yorker* to L.A.'s *Buzz*, these writers know that the white, patriarchal family is no longer the sine qua non of literary experience. What they fail or refuse to see are the deeper changes that cut underneath the skin, into the very marrow of how we perceive the new world we suddenly occupy. Reading itself, and therefore the tiny palace we call culture, is under siege in an age of talk radio, computer games, and especially television, which, like it or not (and the feeling here is NOT), changes the very forms of all communication. Our sense of space is different in an era of cybernetic networks. Our sense of time is different in the age of the sound bite.

Even the political center of the nation-state has been subsumed by that of the multinational corporation. As for the religious verities of the past, forget it.

Rebellion is useless; the times they have a-changed. One young writer I knew told me that he was reluctant to have a character ride in a car because he wanted Charles Dickens to be able to understand his work. This was ludicrous. Dickens did not turn his fertile mind from the factories and counting houses of London to speak to Chaucer. If anything, a true rendering of the changes wrought in everything from what we perceive to the way we perceive to what we believe we perceive (see under: faith) is precisely what Dickens would have wanted to hear from my young friend.

All happy families are different, but each unhappy family is alike in our own way. Literature has always changed with the times. Yet only a handful of contemporary novelists are attempting to explore the transformations of the last half-century. In addition to changes in family structure and shifts in social dynamics, there also has been an upheaval in the philosophical status of thought. Mutability itself may be the most under-acknowledged story of our time—at least in fiction. Since the pace of development is more rapid than it has ever been, the changes that once occurred glacially through millennia have begun to seem so instantaneous as to be discontinuous, and because this is different from all previous experience, those who have not yet been apprised of the changes they personify regard the writers who most deeply reveal this transformative *différance* as chiliastic. The chief lights of this new constellation are Thomas Pynchon, Jonathan Franzen, and Richard Powers. Their work forms a genre that Powers—who most perfectly exemplifies it—has unwittingly already christened "Crackpot Realism."

Soaring past the social, the individual, and the imaginative concerns of earlier literary generations, the work of the crackpot realists takes us into an orbit where the imagination changes the political, the emotional, and occasionally, the physical ground rules of existence. Nor do these works rest content with merely examining such changes; they are usually written in a stylistically overheated mesh-mosh that embodies the distance we've come from E. M. Forster's sad wish, "Only connect," to the phone company's heartfelt "We're all connected." Conspiracies typically form the heart of these novels' plots; though highly implausible, they cannot be discounted as absolutely impossible. So if it could be true, perhaps it must be true. What is conspiracy but the ominous flip side of connection?

The technological wheels of modern life that throw the crackpots are particularly American. They emerged from the laboratories of RCA and IBM as the strategies to promote them came from the boardroom of Time Warner or the war room of the Pentagon. But the crackpot sensibility certainly crops up elsewhere. The example of Salman Rushdie leaps to mind: consider the writer compelled to live an existence of intrigue by virtue of the *fatwah* of a dead cleric—a sort of crackpot ambassador at large. If there are Rushdies in the world, then the genre becomes frighteningly less crackpot and considerably more real. Now take a look at Rushdie's work. Surely children were born somewhere in India at the stroke of liberation's midnight, but the author of *Midnight's Children* insists on the profound meaningfulness of the coincidence. It wasn't merely the contractions of the mother's belly that led to the significant birth; it was the preordained significance of the birth that set off the contractions.

Such a worldview separates the crackpot realists from their literary contemporaries: beyond the welter of random, inchoate experience, they find pattern and meaning. For every code there is a cipher. There's danger and danger's nemesis, truth. If crackpot realism begins with subversion and suspicion, it takes a spiritual journey in a secular rocketship all the way to salvation.

Although they write the quintessential fiction of this age, these novelists do have forebears. Indeed, the first of the crackpots may be Apuleius, who wrote *The Golden Ass* circa 160 C.E., when the remains of Greek faith were contending with newly risen Christianity and the mystery religions of the Levant. In fact, the extraordinary metamorphosis from a man to an ass that is at the heart of the book is undone when Lucius is returned to human form by the goddess Isis. This is not literary game play but an attempt by Apuleius to apprehend the world as he knows it. *The Golden Ass* was written at the moment when Rome was at its apparently invulnerable apogee, but the invisible rot that would eventually destroy the empire had already set in. The question thus arises: Does this sort of fiction emerge at the end of an era—or the commencement of another—a consequence of the struggle to understand the shift in the cultural conversation?

Closer kin to the crackpots include Nathanael West, whose *Day of the Locust* faces the new filmic vision, and, yet earlier, the Gothic novels, especially Mary Shelley's *Frankenstein,* that pathetic tale of technology run amok, and Charles Maturin's *Melmoth the Wanderer,* in which the eponymous hero, more demonic than the simply lustful vampires who succeeded him—from Dracula to Anne "I'm sucking as fast as I can" Rice—ventures into the hidden domain where the virgin and the dynamo meet. Ranging continents and centuries, Melmoth "labors indefatigably, through three octave volumes to accomplish the destruction of two or three souls, while any common devil would have demolished one or two thousand." Quoth the raver, Edgar Allan Poe.

Another crackpot antecedent, Nathaniel Hawthorne, provided the pedagogical underpinnings for this school for difficult children in his introduction to *The House of the Seven Gables.* Deeming his work a "romance," Hawthorne distinguishes it from a novel "presumed to aim at a very minute fidelity, not merely to the possible, but to the probable and ordinary course of man's experience," whereas his own chosen form "has fairly a right to present that truth under circumstances, to a great extent, of the writer's own choosing."

The crackpots' tack of illuminating the real through the fantastic links them to another group of books bound together under the rubric "Magic Realism." When Gabriel García Márquez dared to allow Remedios the Beauty to float away from her spiritual clothesline in *One Hundred Years of Solitude,* it was a scene in literary history that altered the boundaries of the acceptable. It implied that more than representing all of life in a fictional character, this character may experience all that we can conceive. But what Márquez, and since him Mark Helprin, the Israeli writer Meir Shalev, and, perhaps, Toni Morrison have wrought is still rooted in the physical universe, albeit reshaped with an aim to exploring a deeper emotional truth. Again, their folk and fairy tale motifs, while infinitely valuable, are not the truths of the writers' own time, and there is a willful archaism in their fabulism.

Crackpot Realism shatters even Márquez's implicit acceptance of the conventions of plot and character, aspiring to a vastly wider domain. Standing in front of the firing squad, the crackpot realist refuses the metaphorical blindfold that allows the magical realist to declare that life is *like* this. Condemned, he faces the rifles head on, lights a cigarette, and insists that life *is* this. He's not crazy, the world is.

Arriving closer to our destination, we find in postmodernist writing echoes of the crackpots' worldview of chaos and disruption. Born of the sixties, when politics turned weird in Vietnam and the electronic onslaught truly began, the postmodernists jettison artistry, choosing feckless plot and nonexistent character. Maybe that really is the world of MTV, but as MTV itself will not endure, so the postmodernists' dark, glib view implies not only the meaninglessness of their world but of their own labors as well. Donald Barthelme begins one story, "An aristocrat was riding down the street in a carriage. He ran over my father. After the ceremony . . . I was trying to think of the reason my father had died. Then I remembered: he was run over by a carriage." This blasé tautology regarding matters of life and death creates a similar indifference in the reader. After I tossed this book away, I was trying to think of the reason I tossed this book away. Then I remembered: it was stupid.

What this reader has yearned for and suddenly discovered is a literature that faces the absurdity of modern life, as does Barthelme, with the imaginative freedom of Márquez and the seriousness with which Updike pursues his suburban angst. Then, if one adds a pinch of mystical gnosis to the stew, one begins to get the recipe for Crackpot Realism.

It's been twenty-three years since Pynchon's strange, magisterial opus, *Gravity's Rainbow,* opened with the line, "A screaming comes across the sky," and in that time Pynchon's diabolical fantasia has become the daily bread of our lives. We've had Watergate deranging domestic politics, Iran-Contra on the international playing field, and *Star Wars* the movie begetting Star Wars the strategy. Nowadays we all travel the Information Highway together with the convoys of superfluous nonsense that zip at the speed of light via fiber optics into our homes and minds. The science fiction of half a generation ago is the mundane reality of today. Yet the serious, subliminal changes perceived by the lunar vision of the crackpot realist in works such as *Gravity's Rainbow,* Franzen's *The Twenty-Seventh City,* and Powers's *Prisoner's Dilemma* are those wherein a troubled protagonist finds in the external world the embodiment of his own discontent.

The characters in these books are not necessarily lunatics, although they deviate from the standards of normal behavior. It is their authors' perceptions that are clearly askew from common notions of reality. Márquez does not really believe that people fly, but Pynchon may believe that they fuck upon the future landing sites of missiles yet to be launched, and Franzen knows that they plot till they drop.

In *Prisoner's Dilemma,* Powers's Hobson family speaks the dense, elliptical, self-referential dialogue of intelligent people trying to comprehend the bizarre circumstances of their own and every modern citizen's life. The Hobsons are a family with currents as thick as those of Updike's Angstroms, but they have more to think about than sex and mortgages. The traditional, ahistoric novel moves in recurring cycles, but the crackpot realist's universe continually confronts him with the unheard of. The Hobsons must worry about their brilliantly insane father's enigmatic illness (perhaps the result of irradiation by atomic testing?) until page 313 (in the paperback edition), when eldest son Artie realizes the answer to the dilemma posed much earlier by his difficult sire.

The conundrum Artie's father sets forth is as follows: two prisoners are questioned separately. If neither talks, both are sentenced to two years in jail; if both talk, each gets ten years. If one talks and the other doesn't, the talker is freed, the silent one executed. But neither can know how the other will respond to the situation. How then does one act? Artie's midnight realization is that "self-interest is not in the self's best interest. . . . The only reasonable choice was not the choice of reason." It's faith that must stand against logic. Forced to face a situation earlier generations could never imagine in a world redefined by Los Alamos and Disneyland, both of which figure prominently in the book, "Artie named his answer Crackpot Realism."

In the novels of this curious school, the characters, and, by empathic extrapolation, we, the readers, are all prisoners attempting to solve the calculus that leads out of the labyrinth that hems us in. It's not easy. The swirling politics of Franzen's wretched Saint Louis—once the fourth most populous city in the United States, dropped a long way down—are as difficult to penetrate as those of Kafka's *Amerika.* Indeed, Kafka may also be one of the forebears of the form, although he puts his fantasy to a more allegorical use.

In *Strong Motion,* Franzen's second novel, a series of earthquakes is shaking suburban Boston. These earthquakes are caused by the illegal waste disposal practices of Sweeting-Aldren, a large chemical company, whose evil doings are uncovered by the hero, Louis Holland, whose girlfriend happens to be a Harvard seismologist. But what makes this truly crackpot is not merely the grandiosity of the scheme and its ecocosmic effects but the perfect slipknot of strands that goes way beyond the normal coincidences that all fiction, as indeed all life, shares. It's an elevation of random meeting to inevitability. The first earthquake kills one person, Louis's grandmother, who leaves a 22- (as in *Catch?*) million-dollar estate in the form of stock in, you guessed it, Sweeting-Aldren, whose nefarious chief executive is Mr. Stoorhuys, whose son, Peter, is dating Louis's sister. If the reader feels dizzy, imagine how the characters feel. There's also a fundamentalist Christian sect involved.

Plot runs rampant in Crackpot Realism. A geometric rendering of each exemplary novel would show neither realism's straight line nor magic's beauteous curve but an exponentially increasing spiral of paranoia become more bizarre than the paranoid could ever imagine.

Whereas the avatars of minimalism adhere to Peggy Lee's critical dictum, "that's all there is, my friend," the crackpot feels, senses, is certain but cannot prove, that there's more than meets the eye to be understood—IF one finds the evidence missing from the Warren Report or the secret minutes of the Trilateral Commission. If one requires a vile theological animus, there are the Protocols of the Elders of Zion to explain why we're unhappy. Or if one wants a benign Star Chamber passing a benevolent judgment, one can look toward the mysterious MacArthur Foundation, which has wisely chosen to confer its blessings upon Mr. Powers. In any case, there is the assumption that some of us are shaping our world and it's up to Pynchon's Slothrop or Franzen's Martin Probst or Powers's Artie Hobson to discover who. What he requires is a clue, a map, a key.

Metafictionists also try to tease significance from their fictional worlds, but William Gass, Robert Coover, and their ilk seem more interested in the playfulness of words and ideas for their own sake than in the plots their ideas engender. John Barth goes so far as to tell us in the "Dunyazadiad" segment of *Chimera* that the keys to the treasure *are* the treasure. This reduces language to a game. For Salman Rushdie and Richard Powers and his prisoners, the stakes are more substantial. Compelled to stand by the courage of his convictions, the crackpot believes that ideas create his reality; they are vital to breaking the code. Unlike Barth, the crackpot knows that there *is* a treasure and is curiously literal in his literary pursuit. In *The Crying of Lot 49,* Pynchon's pre-*Rainbow* novella involving medieval postal delivery systems, the heroine, Oedipa Maas, has got to break the code, find the secret truth beneath the ostensible truth. She pares away the layers to arrive at the core.

And what is plot but the causal attachments between events?

Return to Hawthorne's preface, and turn the page. We see the title of chapter 1 staring at us: "The Old Pyncheon Family." Accident? Unlikely. Premonition? Conceivable. Positively necessary cosmic link? Of course! You see, it's spooky; there are connections, past and future, among writers, within schools, and between the secret meanings of the world and their literary expositors.

The first place to look for connections is within the language itself. The deadly serious import of alphabets and the grammars they inhabit resound in Crackpot Realism. Words are never "merely" speech; they take on a physical existence as real as their speakers. There are Ernest Hobson's private tapes that construct Hobbstown, an alternate universe within *Prisoner's Dilemma,* and illicit tapes in *The Twenty-Seventh City.* Note, too, the mail scene from Mailer's *The Naked and the Dead,* in which the battle-delayed epistles of the wife of Pacific soldier Roy Gallagher continue to arrive after the telegram announcing her passing. The dead woman is resurrected into a secondary life doomed as the dates on the letters approach the date of her original demise. Until that second death, her words create a life that momentarily triumphs over death itself.

Along with belles or malles lettres, Crackpot Realism is, through its cabalistic fixation on the secret meanings of words, connected to the tiny subgenre of dictionary novels, including David Grossman's *See: Under Love,* in which one character saves his life by telling a series of interconnected fables to a Nazi commandant, and Milorad Pavić's *Dictionary of the Khazars,* in which the different entries provide the solution to a mysterious murder. Both of these books echo the crackpot's universalist concerns in their own lexicographical, Borgesian fashion. The dictionary itself is the map to the completeness that life itself lacks, and if one is clever enough to extract and combine the right words from the *OED,* one can find the answer.

At first glance, this search may appear to be related to trends in recent literary criticism, and to deconstruction's insistence that truth varies according to its seeker's racial, geographical, sexual, or chronological identity, but the crackpot text's ambiguities or uncertainties do not emerge from a relativity of perspective that negates the notion of the absolute; instead, Martin Probst, Franzen's protagonist of probity, probes the dangerous shifting of palpable absolutes. To say that there is no core beneath the parings is nihilistic. Despite despair and tragedy, the crackpot remains secure and therefore optimistic in his faith.

Take faith, as it keeps a tentative fingerhold over the abyss of a world where other values prevail. Most of the crackpot novels are set against a background of military, scientific, or political pandemonium.

From Mary Shelley's high Gothic cultivation of underlying nightmare back to the Visigothic threat that Apuleius intuited massing beyond the boundaries of the empire or beneath the surface of the Pax Romana, we arrive at a turn-of-the-millennium place where conspirators bounce secret messages off satellites to our rooftops, waiting to sweep down, break the rules, and change the universe. If World War I shattered the social compact, opening the door to the radical individual perceptions of Leopold Bloom and his expatriate advocate, Mr. Joyce of Dublin/Trieste/Zurich/Paris, then twenty-five years later World War II rips apart the basic human contract. Moral disintegration is connected to military apotheosis.

The confluence of military strategy and scientific know-how commencing with catapults and battering rams, ambling through steam engines, flew screaming into unity during World War II. That's where it really begins. One older second cousin to the crackpots is wartime novelist Joseph Heller, whose *Catch-22* shares some of the genre's anxieties in a more existential, absurdist fashion. Heller and Mailer, as American soldiers, were the first to hear the whispers of atrocity before the newsreels from Europe incinerated the screens of New York. Of course, their work postdates Bergen-Belsen, but perhaps it takes a generation to translate that unspeakable horror into a literary vocabulary.

Today, the crackpots dive into the underlying madness that created the war rather than the madness of the war itself. Yet none of the preeminent practitioners of this genre to date is Jewish, with the recently surprising exception of Heller, whose new book, *Closing Time,* the sequel to *Catch-22,* in which Milo Minderbinder has become a billionaire arms merchant and Chaplain Tappman has begun urinating atomic heavy water, leaps headfirst into crackpotdom. Not accidentally, *Closing Time* is also the first book in which Heller portrays a realistically Jewish hero, maybe because the crackpot's worldview requires a genetic link to atrocity. In an odd way, the crackpots' is the human response to the Jewish trauma of this century. The Shoah was, partially, the combination of biologically determinist mania, technological expertise, and the chemical effects of Zyklon B. Directly we hear of Powers's outrage at the incarceration of the Japanese-Americans and come to Pynchon's obsession with I. G. Farben, the German chemical cartel that bears a passing resemblance to Jonathan Franzen's Sweeting-Aldren.

Pynchon, the hermit and great hermetic writer of our time, discovers the cartel to beat all cabals, and finally unveils the scale of Evil's endeavors. Yet the I. G. is hardly gone. Ostensibly dismantled after the war, its plants have been reincarnated in Bayer and Hoechst, the international chemical companies that purvey presumably enhancing, potentially ominous "miracle" drugs that change the duration and quality of life, and maybe that's why Pynchon, like Rushdie, must remain hidden. Yet knowledge is power. Despite the enormity of the forces arrayed against any sane definition of humanity, the crackpot realist believes that we can beat these guys if only we can figure out who they are. Perhaps the demonic Melmoth or Herr Dr. Frankenstein's would-be perfect eugenic beast sits on the renamed Farben's Board of Directors.

The scientific element in the crackpots' books may emerge from the nerd mentality, and maybe that's why there aren't many women writers in this club—physics is still more fiercely closed to females than social studies. One imagines an eleventh grade Tommy Pynchon, prematurely reclusive, with a plastic pocket protector to make sure his pens don't leak entropically onto his wash 'n' wear shirt. Given a two-degree turn of fate, one imagines Johnny Franzen, tossing newspapers onto suburban porches, plotting to establish a cellular cable conglomerate, or teenage whiz kid Dicky Powers as a competitor to Bill Gates, computerizing the world. Other hyperkinetic future crackpots flicking spitballs in the back row could be Denis Johnson, *Fiskadoro,* Steve Erickson, *Tours of the Black Clock,* and Michael Doane, *City of Light.*

Certain masters of technology, including Walt Disney and Wernher von Braun, figure as active characters or passive presences in these books, along with the politicians and soldiers who also make cameo appearances. There's Roy Cohn in the form's theatrical analogue, *Angels in America,* and John F. Kennedy in *Libra,* by Don DeLillo, the crackpot family's nervous neighbor and fellow conspiracy buff. References like these are used to lend Crackpot Realism a harder edge than the magical works, which often maintain a sweetness at their core. The authors view the accomplishments of these men through a lens that is colored simultaneously with fascination and abhorrence, thrill and disgust.

The final, astonishing picture that the crackpots draw from the blunt, brutal configuration of dots on their pages still manages to be redemptive, and perhaps that's the greatest miracle of all. Rather than allow themselves to be silenced by the insane energies of willful genocide, they look to perfervidly fecund notions of regeneration. Jonathan Franzen hopes to secure the urban necropolis from further decay through his over-the-edge realpolitik, while Richard Powers moves from Hobbstown to full-scale salvation in his 1993 novel, *Operation Wandering Soul.*

This perhaps fullest expression of Crackpot Realism takes place in and about the children's ward of an urban hospital. A young intern, Dr. Kraft, deals with a host of kids with diseases and mutilations ranging from The Raparrition, whose rhyme-spouting mouth is impaled in a car accident, to the horrifically self-explanatory No-Face, to Nicolino, who ages a decade for every calendar year of his life, to a strange, spiritual Laotian boat girl, Joy Stepaneevong, whose medicine man father has retrieved the silver amulet that fell from the neck of Kraft's own father while the latter was cruising over the jungle in a helicopter gunship for his or his nation's own never fully described covert purposes. It all connects.

Dr. Kraft takes his motley horde to the ballpark while musing on the Crusades. He takes them, including those whose feet don't work and those without feet, dancing. The pain of the children is counterpointed against Powers's overflowing stewpot of meditations on wars, governments, media, mayhem, chaos, and a fantastic rendition of the Pied Piper of Hamelin.

Here is Powers's description of the rats' extravagant passage to extermination that clearly echoes a human death march along a Polish country road:

The crowd—no, the nation, the global confederation of rats—refusing to surrender what is here so excruciatingly close to deliverance once and for all, presses along after him [the Piper] in cold delight. Fortunately the streets have been cleared, road-blocked and flag-routed for this parade catharsis. The waves of wee timorous cowering beasts flow down the street-sluice toward the city walls, lower mammals molded into a molten flood, rats tumbling over rats, surging surflike in curlers and cleansing eddies. But the living flood admits to no shoving, no panic, no collapse of societal mores. . . .

The road becomes a single, continuous file of supplicants on their way to some unimaginable rat holy site. When it dawns on the front ranks of entranced dancers just what potter's field they are posting off to, only the slightest momentary objection ripples through the column. Distress passes; courage revives. . . .

All the way up to the very banks of the Weser, even when the piper stands aside and nothing but the murderous flow of rapids remains between the avant-garde and their arrival, hesitation is briefer than thought and more easily dispatched. The lead rats expand into the watery sacrifice required of them. . . .

Yes, a mother pauses here or there along the bank, thick with plunging bodies brown, and an occasional old retiree breaks into uncomprehending tears as he takes to the drink. But all choose this moment of crystalline clarity, receiving it willingly as opportune, a godsend.

But one last rat pauses, then joins his species in the cleansing, lethal waters: "Reviving at the last possible instant, he surfaces, rights himself in the current, and with his last full measure of devotion pilots his battered body downstream to Ratland, where—the reason he was spared—he prepares a manuscript account, this firsthand report on the proximity of ecstasy to horror."

Somehow, Richard Powers finds comfort. He talks about the "threshold of the opaque" when "things are about to turn," reiterating *Angels in America* playwright Tony Kushner's "threshold of revelation" at this moment when "history is about to crack wide open." The crazed, wishful-thinking crackpot realist has faith in a nature that keeps procreating, renewing itself into further generations of lunacy and murder, trying again and again to get it right. If the last page of any one of these books announces "The End" with terrifying clarity, we turn immediately to the next page 1. Perhaps this time it will read, "A sighing comes across the sky."

Reprinted from TIKKUN MAGAZINE, A BI-MONTHLY JEWISH CRITIQUE OF POLITICS, CULTURE, AND SOCIETY. Subscriptions are $31.00 per year from TIKKUN, 251 West 100th Street, 5th floor, New York, NY 10025.

Impressions of a Paranoid Optimist

Mary Caponegro

The *Review of Contemporary Fiction* is a periodical I esteem most highly; it has been a profound inspiration to me for the last decade, so I couldn't refuse when asked to speak to fiction's status a decade hence, despite feeling insufficiently informed, to say the least. I offer the following highly subjective impressions as a practitioner of fiction who possesses only the meagerest knowledge of hypertext, and nonetheless strong feelings. I'm grateful to the following writers/editors for assisting me through reinforcement and clarification in conversation: David Foster Wallace, Steven Moore, David Weiss, Michael Ives, Bruce McClelland.

AS TO FICTION'S FUTURE (for which I have no crystal ball), I can only say that I have no fear for it; it looks very bright indeed, although the brightness I see is not a technologically produced illumination, such as that which emanates from this framed rectangular glow before me that saves my words as I spew them. That's not the star I'm seeking myself, or being led by, though I feel a certain guilt, an antiquarian-rather-than-micro chip on my shoulder, because I'm yearning for a future that is anything but "istic"; reliant, rather, on a technologically unmediated imagination's endless capacity to augment, transform itself.

It is suddenly old-fashioned, isn't it?—imagination: paradoxically wholesome compared to that more trendy god, technology, who is, in my view, merely tool. Having been raised in a fairly old-fashioned way, I am, I'm afraid, a woman altogether alienated from tools: they intimidate me; I use them tentatively, ineptly, and as a defense, I suppose, I feel they should do me the courtesy of knowing their place. So I find myself stuck in the capacious consolation of an entity that saved me from stagnation in my youth and adolescence and to which I thus give utmost credibility: its name—as if you didn't know—is imagination. I must confess that whenever I think about hypertext, Internet, E-mail—please excuse my naive conflation—I have this retro impulse to crawl into some cave where I can create in darkness and peace and feel primitive, primal, especially *private,* retreat into some contrastingly sensuous *un*virtual reality that produces future as nothing glitzy at all. I want somehow to retreat into body, because that's where I find I locate imagination; the more technologically oriented things get, the more I want to find a physical locus to inhabit in fiction; I can't find an eros in anything else. And from my limited and uninformed perspective, hypertext de-eroticizes fiction. The narrative of my dreams, you see, is one which takes me through plane after plane of pleasure and desire. And when it's done—excuse my metaphorical bluntness—I damn well want to know I've come. Of course I'm talking only about me: *my* fiction, my limits, my vision, my neuroses; I'm writing out of ignorance and only because, truth be told, I was asked to, so let me continue in stating the obvious.

There is something to be said, is there not, for a sensuous reality. There is something to be said for the tactile availability of a letter, an envelope, perhaps with beautiful foreign stamps, within which is sequestered some-one's elegant hand or scrawl, at least signature, a letter you can open, unfold, read half of and tuck in your pocket, hide in your drawer to savor later, or of a book you can read out loud to your partner at night, put a book-mark inside of, feel the weight of in your hand, smell. (I have a colleague who judges books by their aroma; more than cover or photo, he cared solely about how his first published hardback smelled!) Or a voice on the phone, even the voice that you keep hearing on your answering machine represent-ing the person who perpetually eludes you, because it's at least animate, and thus antithetical to the qualities of a world gone ON-LINE. I have no affection for information per se, and consequently no desire to encourage or participate in its apotheosis. I care, and passionately, about a different line; I feel its autonomy must be defended, preserved.

But why so passionate, I must ask myself, why defensive, threatened? Given my own thoroughly un- if not antitraditional fictive proclivities, what's my problem? Am I hypocrite? Or only hyper-crit? How ironic in-deed that what would seem an extrapolation of all I espouse artistically is anxiety if not anathema to me. Let's settle on ambivalence: the word de-fining my stubborn relation, at least thus far, to hypertext. Why is it that the Garden of Forking Paths, once any of them can be summoned instantly by the push of a button—should I say the click of a mouse—ceases to engage me, ceases to be, in any case, my favorite place to stroll? To me, ambiguity is the key; I want a stability fused with instability, like Kafka's Hybrid creature and Odradek. I don't think Borges was after a literal dimen-sion. Isn't that the paradox: that the deconstruction of linearity occurs within the constraints of linear narrative? Without that tension, that disso-nance, I'm bored. Already one has a text that "never reads the same way twice" (Coover); such texts, in fact, have always been my favorite fictions, so why the need to execute, laboriously, the tantalizing implications? Why not simply bask in the overtones? I do know that the space between the screen and elsewhere is the primary site of my own creativity—in-between zones where I move a concept to the "next step." Entrapment in that framed glow precludes opportunity to lie in bed with or sit under a tree with, scribble in the margins of a printed "hard" copy, have the back-and-forth relation that makes fictive friction.

What it all comes down to, I admit, is control; OK, I'm a control freak. Fiction is manipulation, yes? I want to invite the reader in, and while I want anything but a passive guest inside my page, I want also to be mistress of my own hospitality. When the ambiguities shimmer, I'm intrigued, but once each avenue implied is played out to the hilt, the sense of play is dissipated, if not obliterated. One risks feeling that exhaustion of having seen too many rental apartments, of reading too many job applications, and how can you hold them all in mind? And if you can, then what's left to imagine?

Robert Coover, who has taught me a great deal about fiction as well as other profound matters, and who is one of the most eloquent and persuasive advocates of hypertext, says "Much of the novel's alleged power is embedded in the line, that compulsory author-directed movement from the beginning of the sentence to its period, from the top of the page to the bottom, from the first page to the last." The bottom line is that I'm in love with the line, for God's sake. Every sentence probably takes me a week to write. The tension of a finely crafted sentence—one which I attempt to fashion or one which I consume—offers me all the adventure I need—for if I never arrive at closure, to take stock of the cumulative ambiguities "between the lines," how will I know where I am? The prerequisite for residing in these "overtones," it seems to me, is surface closure. Who wants, when it comes down to it, to have all possibilities *literally* available?—any more than you'd want to realize every sexual fantasy. I want this neither when I read nor when I write, nor when I make mundane day-to-day exchanges. (Imagine how exhausting the traffic would be if every such artery were perpetually unclogged!) Some boundaries, some limitations, may be useful. Steve Moore kindly reminded me of a quote from chapter 1 of Thoreau's *Walden:* "We are in great haste to construct a magnetic telegraph from Maine to Texas; but Maine and Texas, it may be, have nothing important to communicate."

I read recently of the soon-to-come (or already available?) mode of research in which one would read an article on Beethoven and, bingo, synesthesialike, hear a sonata. Admittedly seductive, but what, I wonder, happens to the fantasy one now has no opportunity to begin constructing, of what that music *might* sound like, a speculation that would later be challenged, fulfilled or revised by the recording one would hear? In that caesura so much richness lies, it seems to me, and yet we don't think to credit it with any status but inconvenience. And furthermore, what catalysts remain for the imagination when there is no *something contained* in an envelope, or between leaves, behind a cover, the electronic medium not these latter's substitute any more than live music is supplanted by recording: no amount of technical precision serves as substitute for the sensuousness of being in the same space with an instrument, a performer. I suspect a pseudocommunication may proliferate through a technology whose sophistication perhaps exceeds *our* collective sociomaturity—yielding a promiscuity that I'd far rather imagine than participate in. I realize that the cave into which I've crawled brands me a Stone Age fictioneer, but mark my words: years hence we could be looking at a diminution—although no instrument could measure it, and hence we'd not believe it—of the power to hold something in mind *un*realized—a cosmic consequence less overt yet more dire still than carpal tunnel.

But back to the brightness: I do have a more optimistic report; it is not exclusively paranoia I bear. In fact, I can't imagine a more optimistic time for fiction, especially American fiction—when the recent publications of my mentors, friends, and idols alone keep me up to my neck in belles lettres, when I read the few excellent groundbreaking journals that inspire me, such as this one, which has kept me substantively informed ever since I was a student/aspiring writer, connecting me to an avant-garde tradition that I couldn't find much evidence of elsewhere, and which was vital to my education and evolution as a writer.

Even while the publishing industry is proving more and more limited/ing with respect to literary fiction, and great editors are in perpetually precarious positions, and best-sellers are all the marketplace approves/accepts, I think there is an alternate truth, if you will—that enough *is* getting published to keep us engaged and challenged, that language is up to something plenty provocative, and in the same old places it always was, on the page, as well as above/beyond. Meanwhile young writers I'd never heard of emerge by the dozens: new voices that move and excite me, mainstream and non- and in-between. I have the privilege of continuing to publish what I write even though it is not mainstream in the least. I have the privilege of teaching the authors I love, and of teaching young aspiring writers to write *against* the marketplace's limitations.

In my own work I am trying to undertake more elaborate projects, some collaborative, with artists/musicians etc., to push limits, boundaries, of narrative, of reality, in whatever modest ways I can muster. There are probably other worthwhile artistic goals than deconstructing mimesis, but I don't anticipate that one wearing thin for me. I know I will remain primarily a stylist. I am at this moment finishing a collection of stories whose seed was a year's stay in Italy—the last place I ever thought my fiction would take me was to my "roots," but so it did, albeit obliquely; that book was conceived nearly all-of-a-piece but executed in excruciating sequence, a trait I am, alas, unlikely to outgrow. I know that I want story to remain my medium—to continue to explore all the ways I can distort/enhance the form, particularly through comic fiction. My snail's pace is such that I move story by story; a decade probably represents significantly less volume—or should I say fewer volumes?—of published writing for me than for the other writers represented in *this* volume, and in ten years time I will simply be working on that year's story, in much the same manner, I imagine, and I would hope with a still greater depth for the intervening stories. In the end it comes down to sentences, doesn't it? I want only to fashion ever more beautiful elliptical sentences that provoke thought and give pleasure. I'm thrilled to have what audience I have; to me it seems large, and it wouldn't occur to me to measure it against a commercial writer's. I feel fortunate to have begun my career before the worst of this crisis in publishing hit. I'm overwhelmingly gratified that some readers feel stimulated, provoked enough by my work to find it compelling, consoling, intriguing, offensive (or as a friend/fan said to me, "I'd better have another cup of coffee before I try to read that stuff"). I have support, encouragement, the benefit of extraordinary mentors, a marvelous and genuinely literary agent, superb—again literary—editors, as most writers yearn for, places to publish I respect deeply, a way to make a living that allows me to have intimacy with what I love, students who inspire me, everything but enough time to write—but hey, compared to most of the populace that's hardly a complaint. There is plenty to be alarmed about for the coming decade, and deeply alarmed: political conservatism/repression on the one hand, extreme forms of political correctness on the other, and this obviously has an indirect impact on what gets read, published, taught. Education is in great jeopardy; these are things to worry about, but fiction itself will not be impoverished, I don't think; writers will continue to challenge the status quo, continue to transform the complexity of experience, to strive for that elusive, allegedly mythic beast, originality, regardless of the size of their audience in any given decade. Because I teach fiction writing, I know that there are reinforcements on the way, that those of us devoted to the expansion and dissemination of imagination, through whatever various means, are not a dying breed.

Literature as Lyrical Politics

Peter Dimock

> I think we should never write out anything which we do not in-
> tend to commit to memory.
>
> —Quintilian

"WE ARE IN ONE of those moments," a publishing colleague said to me recently, "when nobody knows what is happening." We were talking, as everybody in publishing now must in any conversation lasting more than a few minutes, of the impact of the new media on books and on consciousness. His words came as a relief because they voiced an image that confirmed my uneasy sense that all our talk on this subject had a strangely desperate quality—as if we knew something momentous was happening, but had lost the ability to name what it was we really wanted to talk about, much less decide what we wanted to do.

The comment implied that the technologies mediating our discourse were outstripping our discourse's ability to define those changes or formulate satisfactorily the terms with which to consider and debate their implications. In fact, his comment raises the not unreasonable suggestion that the discourses through which the "selves" and the "we" of our social and cultural interchanges are constituted have come under such intense and transformative pressures in recent years that, temporarily at least, a knowable context for discourse has become impossible.

In this destabilized and destabilizing atmosphere of publishing, I want to make the following straightforward argument: we need to reconnect publishing to the word *public* that is buried within it and to the "live," speaking (or singing) human voice through which any "public" or "people" is constituted according to our literary tradition's founding rhetorical assertion and assumption. That is, I want us to go back and take rhetoric as an organizing system of order, coherence, and community very seriously indeed. (I have come to this formulation and offer this suggestion, for whatever it is worth, as a result of having worked with Barry Sanders as his editor for *A Is for Ox: Violence, Electronic Media, and the Silencing of the Written Word*, published in 1994.)

Such an argument is necessary, first, I think, because it offers a method for specifying the social and cognitive terms in which unlimited access to unlimited amounts of information promised by the new technologies is not equivalent to rhetorical competence. Secondly, this argument is necessary because it offers a way to specify what distinguishes markets for information and entertainment—no matter how responsive, sophisticated, and efficient—from interpretive or "textual" communities. Thirdly, the prospective of the embodied speaking voice, as well as "the public" implied by the circulation of the printed word, is necessary because it can provide a way of specifying how writing and reading matter in the context of the changed human sensorium the new technologies imply and are bringing into being. Finally, such an argument offers a way of framing a sense of literature as a "lyrical politics" in which our discussions can be grounded simultaneously in the individual "citizen-self" as an embodied, spontaneous speaker and the contemporary commerce of symbolic interchange.

I feel some entitlement to speak on these matters because as an acquiring editor it is my business to imagine the contemporary transaction between readers and writers. And because I am an interested party. I am judged, after all, on my successes and failures as a broker of words, and I do have some say in how words are bound, commodified, marketed, and sold. My job no doubt accounts for my being struck increasingly by the thought that publishing now finds itself accountable to two contradictory systems of agency: the rhetorical—that is, that tradition and organization of linguistic resources directed toward action through the arts of verbal persuasion—and the cybernetic—that is, that recent ability through "the application of statistical mechanics to communication engineering" "to replace" "human control functions" through "mechanical and electronic systems" and thereby to organize, determine, and administer the commerce of symbolic interchange according to an instrumental logic not founded by language or rhetoric. (The words for this definition of "cybernetic" are taken, in slightly rearranged form, from *The Random House Unabridged Dictionary,* 2d ed.) In other words, publishing is now going about the business of literature using the new techniques of coordination and control that have in fact superseded a rhetorically grounded and organized structure for coherence and agency. Cybernetics can reproduce all the effects and imitate all the rules of rhetoric, but as a system of order, it is not rhetorical in nature. Indeed, it is, perhaps, what order is freed to become when released from a rhetorical frame of determination.

I want, therefore, to invoke, at the risk of sentimentality, a "lyrical politics of literature" because I think it is essential to recover for our present the memory of the absolute primacy of the embodied, speaking voice as the ground and irreducible reference point for reading, writing, and the book—for our understanding of literature and literacy and as an orientation for our support of literature's sponsoring institutions. I believe we are losing track of the embodied voice speaking autonomously and spontaneously within a socially constructed rhetorical occasion as an absolute ground for coherence and agency. The tradition and institutions of literature assume, I think, this absolute ground of the embodied voice, but they do not specify it because before now they have never had to. Rhetoric simply cannot imagine from within itself the possibilities or determinations of the new technologies. The latter, meanwhile, are perfectly able to duplicate the forms of rhetoric without for a moment being structured by it or held accountable to it.

I do not presume to argue "against" the new technologies. I assume their presence and increasing power. I am arguing for literature as a practice and tradition through which to keep track of and register the fate of the embodied voice under the pressures of the new technologies and the new sensorium they imply. By maintaining touch with the speaking voice as a model of agency and the ground of community that is embodied in the tradition of the book, I believe that literature as an institution can and will, in fact, specify the ways in which the new technologies, for all their possibilities, are also a dispossession.

I realize that what I have said is pitched at a dangerous—perhaps perverse—distance of abstraction. I can only say I hope this is because there is no map for where we are, and abstraction can be useful in specifying our need for one. I take this occasion to advertise two books I believe will prove useful in constructing such a map. One is Barry Sanders and Ivan Illich's *ABC: The Alphabetization of the Popular Mind,* and the other, already mentioned, is Sanders's *A Is for Ox.* Together these books specify, in formally argued, psycholinguistic and historical terms, the ways in which the speaking voice, agency, the written word, and the construction of community and society have been causally intertwined in the West. Their work traces a specifiable psycholinguistic development of Western thought and expression—a specifiable cognitive ecology, if you will, governing the relationships among image, word, and act—that is inextricably tied to the specific rhetorical tradition and culture of print publishing. *ABC* traces the transition of Europe, beginning in the twelfth century, from a predominantly "oral" culture to a literate or an "alphabetized" one. Its argument is made in the shadow of—and to clarify—Illich and Sanders's insight that we ourselves are undergoing a transition of comparable magnitude and importance. Sanders's *A Is for Ox* examines literacy today under the impact of electronic-image culture and the new technologies.

I will not try to summarize fully Sanders's argument. It centers on the proposition that the traditional page and reader (understood as constructed upon the model of the re-voicing and re-staging of rhetorically structured voices) and the electronic screen are fundamentally incompatible instrumentalities of cognition and symbolic interchange. Our electronically mediated culture, he argues, generates ever-increasingly intense and coercive pressures to behave as if they were interchangeable. Sanders tries to show how and why they are not.

I use the adjective "lyrical" because I believe it is the literary form that takes as its domain of experience the moment—and the crisis—in which meaning is created from voiced breath under the impetus of feeling and rhetorical occasion. Its association with "direct feeling" and intense personal expression and with song derives, finally—as the association with Orpheus attests—from the truly liminal and dangerously vulnerable interplay of body, matter, self, other, and society which the creation of meaning through speech represents. In her late poem "Crusoe in England," Elizabeth Bishop says, in Crusoe's voice:

> And then one day they came and took us off.
> Now I live here, another island,
> that doesn't seem like one, but who decides?
> My blood was full of them; my brain
> bred islands. But that archipelago
> has petered out. I'm old.
> I'm bored, too, drinking my real tea,
> surrounded by uninteresting lumber.
> The knife there on the shelf—
> it reeked of meaning, like a crucifix.
> It lived. How many years did I
> beg it, implore it, not to break?
> I knew each nick and scratch by heart,
> the bluish blade, the broken tip,
> the lines of wood-grain on the handle . . .
> Now it won't look at me at all.
> The living soul has dribbled away.
> My eyes rest on it and pass on.

In the last lines we learn that Crusoe (and Bishop) are in a state of permanent mourning for a loved one who has died. That death and the speaker's relinquishment of his own life is signaled by the utter surprise of "Now it won't look at me at all. / The living soul has dribbled away. / My eye rests on it and passes on." The whole poem until now has been a spoken catalog of too-intense, desperately precise observations that registered an all-but-unbearable loneliness. But in retrospect, that catalog suddenly becomes, through the speaking voice, a reciprocity of animated forms brought to animation and into relationship through that voice's animistic powers. Crusoe, on the island, had played Orpheus to the objects of his attention. The powers of that voice, indeed, far outstrip the capacities of its individual user to understand, appreciate, or be made whole by. But the lyric capacity of the human voice is also, as the last lines suggest, always at risk and easy to kill.

Toni Morrison, in her 1993 Nobel lecture, is explicit about contemporary threats to lyric's possibilities. Speaking in the voice of a wise, blind woman, she says,

She is worried about how the language she dreams in, given to her at birth, is handled, put into service, even withheld from her for certain nefarious purposes. Being a writer, she thinks of language partly as a system, partly as a living thing over which one has control, but mostly as agency—as an act with consequences. . . .

[S]he thinks of language as susceptible to death, erasure; certainly imperiled and salvageable only by an effort of will. . . .

She is convinced that when language dies, out of carelessness, disuse, indifference, and absence of esteem, or killed by fiat, not only she herself but all users and makers are accountable for its demise. In her country children have bitten their tongues off and use bullets instead to iterate the void of speechlessness, of disabled and disabling language, of language adults have abandoned altogether as a device for grappling with meaning, providing guidance, or expressing love. . . .

Underneath the eloquence, the glamour . . . the heart of such language is languishing, or perhaps not beating at all. . . .

She is also explicit about the value of lyric. She has the children say, "You, old woman, blessed with blindness, can speak the language that tells us what only language can: how to see without pictures. Language alone protects us from the scariness of things with no names. Language alone is meditation." Then she has the children say:

"Tell us about a wagonload of slaves, how they sang so softly their breath was indistinguishable from the falling snow. How they knew from the hunch of the nearest shoulder that the next stop would be their last. How, with hands prayered in their sex, they thought of heat, then sun. Lifting their faces as though it was there for the taking. Turning as though there for the taking. They stop at an inn. The driver and his mate go in with the lamp, leaving them humming in the dark. The horse's void steams into the snow beneath its hooves and the hiss and melt are the envy of the freezing slaves.

"The inn door opens: a girl and a boy step away from its light. They climb into the wagon bed. The boy will have a gun in three years, but now he carries a lamp and a jug of warm cider. They pass it from mouth to mouth. The girl offers bread, pieces of meat and something more: a glance into the eyes of the one she serves. One helping for each man, two for each woman. And a look. They look back. The next stop will be their last. But not this one. This one is warmed."

I have quoted so extensively from Morrison's lecture because I want to offer an interpretation of it to illustrate my sense of how our culture now uses two finally incompatible systems through which it conducts linguistic and symbolic interchange. The first is rhetorical in nature and intrinsic to the tradition and inheritance of language in the West. The second is cybernetic and is more recent, governed by an instrumental logic inseparable from the new technologies and the vastly increased powers of coordination and administration their application has made possible. I also want to use my interpretation of these passages as a justification for my epigraph that until now, I fear, has been floating a little too freely above what I have been saying.

Morrison, I think, is fully aware in these passages of what happens when words, including these she is speaking, are processed by a logic antithetical to her rhetorical purposes. That indeed is one way of stating the subject of her Nobel lecture: we can hear her words as a way of attempting to preserve the rhetorical occasion of the Nobel Prize as a celebration and defense of the freedom found only through rhetorical craft and the practice of literature against those impinging, seductive, and enveloping forces of celebrity, glamour, entertainment, and power in the midst of which all of us now live our lives. Her words recognize that they themselves provide no defense against their betrayal or subversion by these forces. Words themselves are not proof against anything. Which is why, I think, Morrison constructs her lecture the way she does. Finally, we realize, she is staging the occasion of literature as voiced speech and its lyrical crisis of form, knowledge, and act. At the end, the children's rebuke and plea to the writer turns seamlessly into the narration of the scene I have quoted above. How that moment, that scene, and those words are to be turned into meaning and act is left, at the end, "in our hands."

But two choices are implied: either all this is to be internalized as the unreflecting, inconsequential stimulation of entertainment and decoration through which one passively experiences the present as a consumer of representations and their pleasures or it is to be internalized as a narrative knowledge that has been achieved jointly by the speaker and her audience within a joyful but also dangerous and mutually threatening open, lyrical moment of rhetorical work and interchange.

Which brings me to my epigraph from Quintilian: "I think we should never write out anything which we do not intend to commit to memory." (It is from the *Institutio oratoria,* 10.7, 32. My understanding of its importance and the importance of a rhetorically based understanding of "reading" comes, in part, from Mary Carruthers's wonderful *Book of Memory: A Study of Memory in Medieval Culture,* published by Cambridge University Press in 1990.) I sense that we will truly know the place to which the new technologies have brought us only when we can recover the rhetorical relationship to language underlying an ancient orator's offhand and unremarkable assumption that the written word and the embodied internalization of its rhetorical occasion were inseparable. I interpret both Morrison's Nobel lecture and the ending of her novel *Jazz* as a writer recovering the necessary lyrical and rhetorical basis for literature in order to sustain her art as a form of countermemory to the coercions implied by the substitution of electronic "access" for rhetorical engagement. At the end of *Jazz,* the book itself (like Bishop's knife) speaks:

But I can't say that aloud; I can't tell anyone that I have been waiting for this all my life and that being chosen to wait is the reason I can. If I were able I'd say it. Say make me, remake me. You are free to do it and I am free to let you because look, look. Look where your hands are. Now.

I'll Be Doing More of Same

Jonathan Franzen

THE ACADEMY AS nursing home for terminally ill arts: better that the novel die with honor in the gutter than enter those gates, where candy-striped theorists will offer it the illusion of warmth as they lead it in slow dances, play bingo with it and wink at each other when it roars from its geri-chair about the power it once had. The philistine quotient is probably no greater within the ivory tower than outside it. But it's hard to resist nostalgia for a general audience that expected some entertainment for the money it spent on books; hard not to prefer a system in which wage-earners subsidized good authors for dubious reasons to a system in which tenured professors subsidize dubious authors for good reasons.

For much of this century, the United States had a robust national literature whose audience could with only slight exaggeration be called a general one. There existed such a thing as a novel that Americans who considered themselves civilized found it necessary to have read. For writers, the perception that there was such a thing as a national culture and that a novel could *matter* to it entailed some responsibility to address that culture. And the fact that a significant portion of the population was pursuing culture by buying novels made it possible for ambitious young novelists to imagine writing as a lifelong vocation.

Today, when I try to think of American novelists who might be heeded as a cultural authority, the list begins and ends with Toni Morrison. (If pressed, I might add Saul Bellow, Michael Crichton, Tom Wolfe, and Stephen King.) It's frequently argued, of course, that the country's literary culture is *healthier* for having abandoned the notion of a "general" audience; that a supposedly universal "American" culture was little more than an instrument for the perpetuation of a white, male, heterosexual elite, and that its decline is the just dessert of an exhausted tradition. You hear it said, on college campuses, that there is no America anymore, there are only Americas, that the only thing a black lesbian New Yorker and a Southern Baptist Georgian have in common are the English language and the federal income tax. The likelihood, however, is that both the New Yorker and the Georgian are glued to the Simpson trial on Court TV, that both are struggling to find health insurance, that both have jobs that are threatened by the migration of employment overseas, that both breathe airborne toxins, that both have brothers in the Marines, that both are being pummeled into cynicism by commercial advertising, that both play Lotto, that both dream of fifteen minutes of fame, that both are Democrats, that both are taking Zoloft, and that both have a guilty crush on Uma Thurman. These are aspects of the American experience which until recently it was the job of the novelist to place in a significant, imagination-grabbing relationship with the fears and sorrows of the subjective individual. As welcome as the new diversity among fiction writers is, the task of speaking across (multi)cultural boundaries—the black New York lesbian speaking to a shared reality with a white Southern man, and vice versa—seems more or less to have been abandoned. Abandoned not because of a failure of courage or vision, but because there's simply no longer a home, a stage, a platform for fiction that aspires to be unhyphenatedly "American."

The last ambitious novel of contemporary life to penetrate the national imagination was *Bonfire of the Vanities,* and already, in 1987, Tom Wolfe was struggling to stay half a step ahead of stranger-than-fiction headlines. The successors to Sherman McCoy in the popular imagination have been the creations not of novelists but of "real" life: Claus von Bülow, Ross Perot, David Koresh, Tonya Harding, Kurt Cobain, the Menendez boys, O. J. Simpson—icons whose stories unfold in real time and throw off the occasional spark of generic significance (Populist Rebellion, Teen Alienation, Race in America) but in the main are pure spectacle, unmediated and unmeaning. Obviously, our country prefers its stories in this form; natural selection, whose modern forum is the marketplace, has favored Lorena Bobbitt and River Phoenix over Rabbit, Yossarian, and Garp. As a novelist, however, I see in this preference a grievous loss. I consider the fictional Jay Gatsby not only more representative of his age and of the American experience than the literal Charles Lindbergh, but vastly more expressive of the paradoxes of human existence in general.

Technological consumerism is an infernal machine. The American writer today faces a totalitarianism of commercial culture analogous to the political totalitarianism with which two generations of East Bloc writers had to contend. To ignore it is to court irrelevance. To engage with it, however, is to risk writing fiction that makes the same point over and over: technological consumerism is an infernal machine, technological consumerism is an infernal machine. . . . In the face of this overwhelming new circumstance, this damming and draining of the literary mainstream by the Corps of Cultural Engineers, I see the remaining trickle of literary production following three likely courses as it makes it way into the Gulf. The first and most vital is the new tribalism—gay, lesbian, African-American, Asian-American, and Latino writers writing for audiences in search of self-understanding. Identity politics may itself ultimately foster its own kind of totalitarianism, but at least it's a refreshing change from McLife in America; and by cultivating a new generation of readers, writers like Terry McMillan, Jessica Hagedorn, Dorothy Allison, and Amy Tan are doing us all a favor.

Then there's the picturesque arroyo of fiction produced and consumed by academics—a desertscape of nostalgia, mediocrity, and pomo brow-furrowing, the vast bulk of it neither more harmful nor less skippable than the poetry that fills our smaller journals. No doubt we can expect to see a further increase in "lyrical" novels published by university presses and featuring grad students and college profs as protagonists. A more dismal trend is the growing critical infatuation with "revolutionary" technologies and the "subversive" side of pop culture. As long as there was such a thing as a literary mainstream, the inhospitable wetlands of the avant-garde served a purifying purpose. The writers who shaped the popular imagination could draw on that fund of formal experimentation, that expansion of the allowable, that dredging up of riverine human muck: that bohemia. And how refreshing it was, after nearly drowning in the bigness of Bellow or Mailer, to take refuge among Hawkes and Burroughs. But when the avant-garde is all that remains—when the rebels who kept the establishment honest are themselves enshrined as the establishment—we're left without an opposition. I see an academy (and foresee a national literature, produced by academics) lost in fantasies of transgression and subversion that are likely only to confirm for young people, who have a keen sense of bullshit, the complete irrelevance of literature. I often feel that the single most tonic thing we writers could do for this country's literary life would be to publish half as many novels and teach twice as many literature courses, if only to displace an equivalent mass of theorists who have forgotten why novels get written and why people who aren't Ph.D. candidates might care to read them.

Finally, there's the old channel of commercially viable literary fiction, to which the spring and fall publishing seasons continue to bring flash floods as various reliable thunderheads (Stone, Roth, Morrison, Smiley, Updike, Oates, etc.) release their loads; for a few weeks you can stand on the banks and see the literary river in the fullness of its former beauty. I have grave doubts, however, about the audience for fiction like this. My gut sense is that its median age is pushing sixty and will be dropping off the edge of the actuarial table any year now. Certainly the conventional publishing wisdom is that a novel by a non-name-brand author now has to be fairly high-concept to attract the attention of the scattered remnants of the once-"general" audience. Hence the forecast for the mainstream calls for increasing filmability, simplicity, and brevity; no young Gaddises or Barths need apply.

So what will become of us writers who are old enough to have cut our teeth on Dickens and Proust and *The Recognitions* and *Gravity's Rainbow* and to have tailored our self-definitions accordingly, but are young enough to be facing obsolescence before retirement age? High concepts have begun to give me nosebleeds, and my feelings about the academy are self-evident. Worst of all, I'm untribal. Or rather, my personal tribe of white American men is too busy making money or being depressed over not making money to have time for tribal tales of business and depression. I have a suspicion, in fact, that my tribe was *never* much interested in tales of itself, that the "general" audience our national literature once possessed was always predominantly female, and that sometime around 1973 women finally got tired of getting their news of the world via (frequently misogynist) male perspectives, and that that was the end of the "general" audience.

So who am I writing for and why am I doing it?

If fiction à la Dickens, Proust, and Pynchon is indeed being rendered obsolete by the media revolution, it's because such fiction's axioms and fundamental enterprise are likewise being rendered obsolete. I'm assuming, here, that most works of serious literature share certain things: a belief in the individual; a "pessimistic" conviction that the world (or history, or fate, or God) will be forever smarter than the people in it; a commitment to mediating between the author's subjectivity and the world in which she finds herself by subjecting that subjectivity to the rigors of conventional form and permanent language; and the whole battery of stuff like honesty and responsibility and love and significance that constitutes "humane values."

If you believe in these humane values, it's possible to continue believing in literary fiction as, if nothing else, a vessel for preserving them, i.e., for maintaining some semblance of their relevance. And there are two ways you can believe in fiction. You can believe in it despairingly, the way dying people believe in God even though God clearly won't save them; believe in it, that is, simply because of faith's capacity to ennoble and enable, to give meaning and beauty to life. Or you can believe in it on the more rational ground that the incipient Media Age, for all its self-serving claims to being tomorrow's hegemony, seems not particularly likely to sustain itself for more than a generation before succumbing to its internal contradictions and harmful side effects.

To the extent that this Media Age doesn't affect my work as a novelist, I'm optimistic. To the extent that it does affect my work, I can't help pointing out that the problems it presents the literary world are nowhere near as serious as the ones it presents the real world: human isolation, fragmentation, the acceptability of demanding instant gratification, rising tides of illiteracy and depersonalized violence, the spectre of vast unemployment at the hands (as it were) of robots and computers, and maybe especially the demolition of responsible political discourse in a "self-governing" nation and the consequent growing potential for demagoguery, racial war, and financial catastrophe. In the face of problems like these, it's hard to get too excited about the decline of sales in hardcover art fiction. Or, conversely, about the interesting new world of hypertext or the explosive growth of data sources and various interactivities (which nobody has yet convinced me that human beings will find time in their short days to make use of). Even the most out-there fiction writers like Gaddis and Pynchon and DeLillo are bent on affirming an old verity: that the formal, aesthetic accounting of the human plight is redemptive.

The fact that critics and analytically minded fiction writers have lately discovered a "crisis" of form may not mean that printed fiction has exhausted itself, but simply that an era of (critically privileged) formal innovation is coming to an end, and that the time has come for form's dialectical counterparts, content and context, to return as the vectors of the new. I believe that writers with "new" content have relatively little interest in, and a whole lot of skepticism toward, the technological blessings with which the market economy is showering us. Who wants to look to the future when every laptop-toting junior exec is looking to it and angling for his share of the profit? What self-respecting artist in Germany in 1935 was interested in celebrating the really fascinating changes that were sweeping German culture? When the times get really, really awful, you retrench; you reexamine old content in new contexts; you try to preserve; you seem obsolete. Think of Mandelstam, Akhmatova, and Brodsky continuing, in the belly of the Soviet beast, to write of nature and the human heart. The day comes when the truly subversive literature is in some measure conservative. Maybe it's time for us to ask ourselves whether apocalypse might be a self-indulgence.

Bad Times

Janice Galloway

THERE IS A PLACE called the Centre for Contemporary Arts in Sauchiehall Street in Glasgow, a gallery space, theater and performance café sort of affair where the newest of new artistic work is not only permissible but expected. It is a welcoming place: interested, broad-minded, eclectic. Exhibitions staged there seem to assume that's what the people who come to see them are too.

A few months ago now, I did a reading at the CCA as part of a season called Bad Times: an exploration of how artists in different fields treat the subject of depression, suicide, political lean times and mean times—bad times, I suppose. I was pleased to be invited and enjoyed the reading but that is not the subject of this essay. The subject of this essay concerns the week before, when a journalist phoned me. I had one hand hauling wet stuff out of the washing machine, the other restraining a three-year-old and the phone under my jaw, but I was polite. I made time to listen. He didn't want to talk about the reading, he said. He wanted to talk about *concepts*. Fine, I said. So, he said: what did I think about all this depression and suicide business. I didn't understand the question. This nineties vogue for despair, he added helpfully. I still didn't understand the question. Well, isn't it all a bit self-indulgent? he said, lumping a lot of misery and neuroses together and calling it Art?

Now I won't pretend everything fell into place at that moment but it should have. He wasn't asking questions at all, he was suggesting dismissal: offering me a choice between reaction and complicity. I struggled on with him for a while but the subsequent article, its references to something vaguely termed "the uplifting," its demand for an art that "looks on the bright side and away from the relentless focus on the sordid" confused me for days. I had been to the exhibitions, I had thought the work wonderfully thought-provoking. His refusal to look at the work on the grounds that there are some things better not discussed or better left out of Artistic dialogue (the old "appropriacy of subject matter" chestnut) was something I was not prepared for. I was shocked. I lost sleep. Worse, I couldn't work out why. I was seeing nothing new. Attempts to silence certain subjects or voices and render them "beyond the pale"—by ridicule, ostracism, pretending they aren't there, or any other method—are hardly unfamiliar tactics; while elitist canon-making and the promotion of some ideas as "right" or "real" at the expense of others which are "forbidden" or "invalid" are everyday realities. The only reasons I could come up with for my unpreparedness were (a) this right-wing, repressive norm intruding on the "safe" space of the CCA, and (b) (less reasonably) the fact the journalist was younger than me. Neither are valid excuses. I should not, I realized after some time to think, have been shocked or even surprised at all.

It is, surely, uncontentious to say that the dominant context for everything and everyone for the past umpteen years, at least as far as those who govern us are concerned, is that of the "marketplace." All levels of government and media are so saturated in the language, concepts, and priorities of this "marketplace" that it is becoming harder to avoid taking its language and priorities as givens, i.e., not open to question. The central idea, crudely, conflates MONEY, POWER, and WORTH, making this trinity the ultimate test of the "common sense" or "reality" of all else. Thereafter, market philosophy is reliably devoid of metaphor. Phrases like "good investment" can usually be taken literally: invisible or abstract "return" is regarded in much the same way astronomers regard astrology—not only wrongheaded but humorously medieval. Thus balancing books, supply and demand, and hard cash are empirical proofs, i.e., "real things"; while Human Happiness, the Common Good, and Morality are rendered pale pink wooly ideas harking back to a "less competitive," i.e., stupid age.

From here, several other things follow. It follows, for example, that moneys spent on things that do not reap literal return is not "commonsensical." Public spending cuts become "realistic" and even improving. Education, for example, is "best served" by funding which furthers "necessary" grading exercises for employers, and elsewhere "rationalized" by cuts. Further Education, likewise, "joins the real world" when funds go on "vocational training" and cuts are applied to "Arts and recreation." Public Health is "streamlined" and "strengthened" by cuts while Welfare cuts "help define areas of real need." By extension, social conscience becomes "trickle-down economics"; the highest morality is "good housekeeping"; active mutual citizenship becomes individual consumer rights, and knowing the price of everything and the value of nothing goes by the name of "sound business sense." This is generally sold to the British public by appeals to tightening-of-belts, pulling-of-selves-together, and invocations of the Dunkirk spirit. The *lumpenprole* are meant to understand why there is no jam today (and why those with jam already are to get more) if they are told some will "trickle down" to them tomorrow. And so far, at least with the Southern English population, it's seemed to work very well indeed.

Where Art fits is, simply, uneasily. There's a sort of received wisdom in all elitist hierarchies that Art, like Guinness or perhaps medicine, is "good for you"—not just because you can make it into plays that bring in tourist revenue, but in other, less definable ways. Words like *edifying* pop unbidden into otherwise "sensible" heads. Art is a refining influence, full of lofty ideas about aesthetics and the human condition. It is generally held to be "a marker of civilized society" and having some of it around makes everything look a little more . . . well . . . humane. (One of Mrs. Thatcher's greatest failings, according to the old-guard right, was that she was "a crashing Philistine," which lowered the tone uncomfortably for those who think ruling elites ought to prefer Wagner rather than Andrew Lloyd Webber with their policy-making.) Even so, we mustn't get carried away. Lofty ideas are not (polite cough) the same as practicalities, which is to say Art is all very well but not essential. Essential, that is, in the way the needs of private industry and MP's expense accounts and government PR exercises and increases in the salaries of judges and so on and so on are. It is, after all, PROFIT that makes the "real world" go around. Art must not get ideas above itself. Art is only icing: Business is the cake.

Now, if you think Art is fundamentally important to human beings—not as a notion but as a practical reality—the present anti-artistic (i.e., anti-humanist) thrust of the present party-political climate has to be worrying. Art is not decoration, or something pretty by someone dead. It's not escapism or entertainment. I'm not saying there is anything wrong with any of these things but they're not Art. Art is more even than ideas. Art is the *exploration* of ideas: an attempt, I think, to make sense of the experience of being human through a process of creative skepticism. This in turn means Art is best at work when it's being prickly, querulous, and hostile to complacency of thought. It is obvious how Art itself is a problem for the new right: too many questions do not sit well with the smug face of an apparently immovable government. You don't, however, need to issue *fatwas* or offer jail sentences instead of awards to attempt to limit Art. The hierarchical, undemocratic givens of power-politics can do it a whole variety of much subtler ways, up to and including denial of access to any means of dissemination or even denial that it exists (exactly what happened to the creative work of women for centuries—and arguably still does), or by suggesting that some kinds of subject matter are "out of bounds." It can provide only an impoverished education to the bulk of its citizens, leading them to think that's all education is. It can withdraw publicity, access, and funding from certain kinds of work and propagandize as "worthwhile" the stuff that makes fewer waves or challenges only at a trivial level. Or—the one our present government seems to be pinning a good many hopes on—it can stress private sponsorship as the way forward for funding, effectively encouraging artists to self-censor for fear that any potential sponsor will deny funding if they're too "difficult" or "controversial." And while there are some private sponsors who wouldn't dream of laying down an agenda for any creative artist, we surely delude ourselves if we do not acknowledge that the "Art" most likely to "win" sponsorship will probably be at the already established, "safe bet" end of the artistic spectrum. The work of unknown composers or writers, anything deemed too experimental or unorthodox or "geared to a minority audience" or—and here we come full circle—too depressing, will be consistently starved of funds and dissemination. This is not only a recipe for encouraging work of the bland-est sort, the kind that can be consumed for "relaxation" with a guarantee of no unpleasant aftertaste, but it also blunts the cutting edge of the most radi-cal of new artistic work, the very work that opens the fresh ways of seeing on which all Art thrives. In short, what we are more likely to encourage by forcing the market model as suitable to assess the worth of creative work is an endless recycling of the same old warhorses for fear of doing anything that might fail in box-office terms (Carnegie and Albert Halls, are you lis-tening?), work stagnant for want of radical input, work that no longer chal-lenges or stimulates exploration of ideas, which means Art reduced to the decorative or the entertaining, which is to say NOT ART AT ALL. Maybe one can expect nothing more of a government that is so spiritually bankrupt it sees nothing ironic in hinging the notions "Art and Heritage" together as a government department, but it's awful anyway.

Once I had thought all this through, the journalist who spoke to me, his questions, their tenor and assumptions, began to look more understandable. I had simply not taken into account how much the pattern of repressive thinking had progressed in the last few years but now I was forced to look again. In Britain, after more than fifteen years of single-track policy-mak-ing, a whole new generation who cannot remember alternatives to "market-place" meretriciousness is coming to fruition, and that, surely, has an effect on how younger people view what Art (and people) are. Disaffection (of various sorts, from a *que sera* attitude to a drug culture to a strong sense of political impotence to the notion that individual rather than collective action is the only possible form of protest) and born-again, quasi-nostalgic repressiveness are the two most prevalent manifestations I can come up with. Both are obviously evidenced in the body of new British writing and writers, though the latter, in the guise of saturated tolerance ("ENOUGH IS ENOUGH do we really need to have our noses rubbed in this kind of thing is it supposed to be modern and if so call me old-fashioned" etc.), is the one that finds most favor with our critics. I know of course there always have been and always will be attempts to control what artists do, sugges-tions from noncreators about what "true" creation should consist in. The present reactionary tendency, however, is more blatant and shameless than anything I can remember and the more shocking for its coming after Barthes, Foucault, Russ, Spender, et al.—i.e., great schools of thought that seemed to be beginning to democratize how we view and codify art. And it is in that, I guess, the worst of the shock resides. Mr. Major's inane BACK TO BASICS* slogan and his more recent advice to "condemn more and

---

*The current rumor in this country that the BACK TO BASICS slogan was thought up by Barbara Cartland is telling: the romantic novelist was quoted in the *Observer* as saying, "Nothing is allowed to be nice any more: everything has to be sordid"—simply a cruder version of what the journalist who called me was saying. This time it's younger rather than older fogeys who are promoting the repressive bloody nonsense.

understand less" are, it seems, becoming our critical and artistic climate too. The apparent obverse—the kind of criticism that stresses appearance and novelty (and advances paid) rather than the ideas explored in a book—isn't: it's simply "marketplace" values in thin guise. From young women who deny their sex both in their writing and with statements about "being a writer, not a woman" for fear of sounding upsettingly "feminist" to young men who write about sex by objectifying and denying sexuality because anything else is too "politically correct"; from out-of-the-woodwork academics yearning for "the voice of restraint" to elitist critics and criticism that would condemn work for its subject matter or language being "upsetting" or "too experimental" or "last year's thing"—the absurd wish for God to be in his heaven and all simple with the world again (i.e., the way it was before we knew all this politically aware stuff) seems overwhelming. It is worrying, it is distracting, it is confidence-sapping. Most of all, it is irrelevant. I've stopped buying papers and no longer watch TV. I do still go to see exhibitions I like and watch for what the papers ignore. I try to remember that things get worse before they get better and think it's really no worse than it was in the nineteenth century. The best of our art was unlikely to be promoted, funded, or encouraged then either but it was still there. Even so, the nineteenth century had more excuses. These are uneasy times and it would be an act of the worst *mauvais foi* to fall for the comforting tosh that "Art (or tolerance or inclusiveness) will out" let alone triumph. Katherine Ann Porter's splendid avowal

I have no patience with the idea that whatever you have in you has to come out, that you can't suppress true talent. People can be destroyed; they can be bent, distorted and completely crippled. . . . In spite of all the poetry, all the philosophy to the contrary, we are not really masters of our fate . . .

says it right for me too. What we can do, however, is learn a little about our limitations. I've already learned to be much more careful about who I spend time with on the phone. We can keep in touch with each other, pick up survival techniques, keep our eyes open, be suspicious, conserve our energies to keep producing work we can confidently call Art.

Slouching towards Grubnet:
The Author in the Age of Publicity

Gerald Howard

> "To write—was that not the joy and the privilege of one who had an urgent message for the world?"
>
> —Marian Yule in *New Grub Street*

> "There's no question of the divine afflatus; that belongs to another sphere of life. We talk of literature as a trade, not of Homer, Dante, Shakespeare . . . I mean, what on earth is there in typography to make everything it deals with sacred?"
>
> —Jasper Milvain in *New Grub Street*

I WAS IN THE MIDDLE of reading literally my seventeenth article on Martin Amis's *The Information* and all the chattering class controversy surrounding its publication, quite a good one in *New York* magazine by James Kaplan, well in the upper tier of such articles (and by then I had become a connoisseur), with, amazingly, a new spin on its subject (Kaplan plays tennis with Amis as a journalistic device to explore envy and competitiveness between writers, *The Information*'s big preoccupation), when I turned the page and confronted the picture, or, as I have come to think of it, The Picture. The photographer at the New York publication party for *The Information*—a major league see-and-be-seen event for the buzzoisie, you can be sure—had captured four scribbling bad boys, American literary outrage Bret Easton Ellis, British literary outrage Will Self, transatlantic literary neo-Gothicist Patrick McGrath, and the man of the hour himself, Martin Amis, each at precisely the moment when the party mask slips to reveal the soul beneath the skin. On the left was Ellis, his nascent jowls reminiscent of Richard Nixon during his Checkers period, his eyes showing alarming areas of white in the manner of Tor Johnson, the wrestler/actor of Ed Wood's stock company. On the right were Self, tall, pin-striped, cigarette in hand and profile both thrust aggressively forward, his forehead marred as if allegorically by a boil, and McGrath, smug expression and comfortable bay window proclaiming the pleasant fruits of his skillfully creepy fiction. In the center, famously shorter than the others, was Amis himself, with his drink and hand-rolled fag, his often handsome face seemingly caught in mid-morph into some sort of reptilian visage. The snapshot spoke of near-toxic levels of ambition and self-regard, constant crosschecking for position in the full glare of the media spotlight—the Wildean ravages, perhaps, of having one's name set in boldface too often. Success—and by local community standards these men were very successful indeed—in the literary purlieus of the nineties clearly did not convey grace and spiritual health. The photo's miasmic air proclaimed, in its own sly way, that being a novelist, even one whose name was on the lips of every literary saloniste and cocktail party-goer, was no ticket to dignity and no anodyne to status anxiety. It said clearly, at least to me: Mother, don't let your son grow up to be a novelist. It begged the question, at least of me: Would I trust these people with any portion of my inner life?

Which were, of course, the clearest message and biggest question any dispassionate reader might take away from *The Information* itself. Amis's novel might be described as a demonstration of the proposition that hatred of one's peers is so powerful a force in the literary world that they can cause writers to behave approximately like Tonya Harding. A brilliantly knowing and occasionally hilarious *tour d'horizon* of the postliterate literary landscape, from the badly appointed low-rent districts to the gaudy, gilded precincts of bestsellerdom, *The Information* paints a largely accurate picture of that world—if you discount the possibility of art and transcendence and any sense of what these qualities might mean, how they might manifest themselves.

The Information itself may or may not be art, but it was certainly a prime postmodern instance in the dizzying circularity with which the book's whole publication saga mirrored its themes of venality and inauthenticity. In as abbreviated a form as possible, and with apologies to readers who have heard all this before: Having written a novel hinging on a failing writer's midlife crisis, Amis, himself in midlife (though hardly failing), proceeded to act out his own. He left his wife and children for an American heiress (nice touch, that) and subsequently presented his longtime publisher Jonathan Cape with a stunning demand for £482,000 for his new book. Some claimed that the money was needed to pay for an extensive and expensive new set of teeth from an American dentist (nice touch, that). Then certain of Cape's authors, demonstrating the effect of financial envy, cried foul in the public prints, precipitating a tabloid frenzy. At some point in the protracted negotiations Amis ditched his longtime literary agent for a notoriously rapacious American one nicknamed "The Jackal" by the British press (nice touch, that). As it happens, Amis's old agent is married to his oldest and closest literary mate (and tennis partner), Julian Barnes; the friendship did not survive the business rupture and the gossip that the best-selling hack who is the butt of most of the novel's jokes was modeled on Barnes himself. In any event, Amis ended up selling his book to HarperCollins for just about the same sum as Cape had offered, leaving behind him the scorched earth of romantic, literary, business, and fraternal associations. As his former agent, sibyl-like, observed, "The ironies of this outcome will be lost on none of the participants."

This whole farrago stopped the British literary-industrial complex in its tracks for weeks and became a national obsession of O. J. Simpson-like proportions. Similar to that murder and its aftermath, it involved a dizzying loss of perspective in which foreground and background, subject and object, became hopelessly confused—a Mongolian cluster-fuck of reality and fiction, art (or "art") and life. So inescapable was the ubiquitous information about *The Information* that one wag, when asked at a dinner party whether he'd read the book yet, replied, "Well, yes—but not *personally.*" *The Information* the book and *The Information* the pseudo-event both provide rich texts in which we may descry the strange warpings of character, the necessary mutations in the figure of the author in a world in which, cf. Colin Powell and Newt Gingrich, a book tour can become a proxy for a presidential campaign or a national political debate.

I myself *have* read *The Information* personally, and in my view Martin Amis's powers of provocation exceed his powers of literary invention; nothing in the novel quite reaches the deliciously ironic peaks of its path to publication. Still, it is a sharply observed, consistently amusing, and sourly well-informed insider's view of the authorial experience in an age when a book is as often as not the pretext for everything *except* reading. Its hapless antihero Richard Tull personifies every flavor of literary futility. A "marooned modernist," his novelistic career has ground to a shuddering halt. His latest work, *Untitled,* "with its octuple time schemes and rotating crew of sixteen unreliable narrators," is so unreadable as to induce migraine headaches in all who attempt it. He ekes out a precarious living as an editor at a vanity press, a man of all work at the impecunious *Little Magazine* ("it really did stand for something in this briskly materialistic age. It stood for not paying people"), and a second- to third-tier reviewer of second- to third-rate literary biographies like *The Soul's Dark Cottage: A Life of Edmund Waller* and *AntiLatitudinarian: The Heretical Career of Francis Atterbury.* He is impotent with his attractive wife and his unattractive mistress, and he spends his days grinding his teeth over the unaccountable success of his quondam best friend, novelist Gwyn Barry, and plotting increasingly baroque and ineffectual forms of revenge.

As Richard Tull's career describes a relentlessly declining arc, Gwyn Barry's follows an infinitely and perplexingly ascending trajectory towards an empyrean of extraliterary fame, smug fatuity, and swollen royalty checks. His painfully sincere and modishly multicultural utopian fantasies *Amelior* and *Amelior Regained* have enjoyed a stupefyingly inexplicable success similar to that of Robert Waller's *The Bridges of Madison County.* (Tull muses bitterly, "*Amelior* would only be remarkable if Gwyn had written it with his foot. Why was *Amelior* so popular? Gwyn didn't do it. The world did it.") As a result Barry enjoys all the trophies of the blockbuster brand-name author: the sexy upper-class wife, the lavish household, the constant barrage of attention from every medium, the shortlisting for lavishly remunerative literary prizes with names like the Profundity Requital, the triumphal book tours planned with the precision and the similar intent of amphibious landings. Richard Tull accompanies Barry on one of these tours across America to promote *Amelior Regained,* assigned to write a personality feature on his friend that will "examine the pressures facing the successful novelist in the late 1990s." The forced march through the talk-show archipelago that America has become sparks anti-epiphanies like this for Tull:

The contemporary idea seemed to be that the first thing you did, as a communicator, was come up with some kind of slogan, and either you put it on a coffee mug or a T-shirt or a bumper sticker—or else you wrote a novel about it. . . . And now that writers spent as much time telling everyone what they were doing as they spent actually doing it, then they would start doing it that way round too, eventually.

Everywhere he travels with Barry Tull observes "the excitement of increase, of reputable profit, the kind you get when commerce meets art and finds it good."

Something of that same excitement surrounded *The Information* itself. Amis clearly intended it as his Big Statement on the darkening cast of life at the end of the millennium and the ineffectuality of literature in the face of these developments. The book suffers from its ambitions: too many passages show the rhetorical strain of overreaching for the cosmic; the thugs Tull enlists in his revenge schemes are entirely too literary in conception to be remotely convincing; and similarly Tull and Barry are too extreme in their haplessness and self-satisfied cluelessness respectively to move beyond the scope of skillful cartoons into the autonomy of fictional characters. And there is something, well, unpleasant and creepy about Amis's worldview. Famously precocious as a young literary editor and novelist, his is the nasty, practiced cynicism of the smartest kid in the class, and his corrosive view of the literary life is served up with a smirk that implicitly excludes himself from any taint of Tulldom or Barryness.

I spoke to a young writer of my acquaintance about *The Information,* someone just launched on his own career. I was curious how he might weather this putative portrait of the life that awaits him. Not well, as it happens. He complained of the book's "weird conflation of vileness and success" and said that reading it made him feel "like I'd received a blood transfusion from a lizard." He said that "writers put enormous effort into sandbagging their internal levees against a rising internal tide of bitterness and recrimination" and the book felt like a flood of such feelings overflowing their banks. When I asked him whether he agreed that envy was as powerful a force in writers' lives as the novel maintains, he said that in their heart of hearts writers were as envious and competitive, but in their soul of souls they were warm, generous, helpful, and giving. In this regard *The Information* has a cold heart—and no soul at all.

Still, before we dismiss *The Information* as the product of both a notoriously catty and insular literary culture and a notoriously cynical literary intelligence, we need to look more closely at the literature of contemporary authorship in America. Here, too, reassurance for writers and readers is hard to find, offering as it does conspicuous examples of an emerging literature of disgust.

Consider *Wonder Boys* by the much-heralded young writer Michael Chabon, published at about the same time as *The Information* and as ethnographically accurate a portrayal of the campus-centered American literary scene. Its narrator and Richard Tull equivalent is Grady Tripp, a novelist similarly mired in dismal midlife and midcareer. A college writing teacher, divorcé and morose pot enthusiast, Tripp is tethered to a dying novel called *Wonder Boys,* a vast family saga that, on the morning that he is driving to the airport to pick up his impatient book editor for WordFest—one of those alarmingly overproliferated literary festivals—stands at 2,611 pages. (Cf. Richard Tull: "One of the many troubles with his novels was that they didn't really get finished. They just stopped.") Belying its jaunty tone and skillfully farcical plot, *Wonder Boys* is littered with casualties of the literary life. Contemplating them (and himself), Tripp muses:

> I . . . began to wonder if people who wrote fiction were not suffering from some kind of disorder—from what I've come to think of . . . as the midnight disease. The midnight disease is a kind of emotional insomnia; at every conscious moment its victim—even if he or she writes at dawn, or in the middle of the afternoon—feels like a person lying in a sweltering bedroom, with the window thrown open, looking up at a sky filled with stars and airplanes, listening to the narrative of a rattling blind, an ambulance, a fly trapped in a Coke bottle, while all around him the neighbors soundly sleep.

Were this to get out, Breadloaf and numerous other literary sleepaways would become ghost camps. Predictably, Tripp's editor Terry Crabtree, a man with his own set of problems ("I'm hanging by, like, three molecules of thread at Bartizan"), finds *Wonder Boys* too burdensome to take on. "I need something fresh. Something snappy and fast. Something pretty and perverted at the same time." Chilling words that will resonate alarmingly with fourth novelists everywhere.

The prodigiously talented novelist Richard Powers betrays much the same dismay at the internal costs of his vocation in startlingly intimate terms in his latest book, *Galatea 2.2.* Running parallel to a Shavian plot involving the literary and sentimental education of a post-HAL computer entity named Helen is a comprehensive account of Powers's own publishing history, complete with actual review excerpts—a grim testament of pained composition, gnawing dissatisfaction, critical misapprehension, and creative exhaustion. He dismisses his first novel, *Three Farmers on Their Way to a Dance,* as "no more than a structured pastiche of every report I'd ever heard from C. [Powers's lover] or abroad," and his fourth, *Operation Wandering Soul,* as "an ornate, suffocating allegory about dying pedes at the end of the century." Granted a year's residence at a Midwestern university, Powers shuttles between the computer techies, who promise (or threaten) to create intelligences and even sensibilities equal to any mere novelist's in scope and penetration, and the English department, whose reigning orthodoxies proclaim the death of the author, the illicit privileges of the text, the infinite variability of meaning. His immersion in cognitive neuroscience, the actual mechanics of the brain's workings, provokes less wonder than paralyzing self-consciousness. Not surprisingly, writer's block lurks: "nothing waited for me on the far side of story's gaping mountain. Nothing but irremediable Things As They Are." Powers's "my fair software" adventures with Helen are wonderfully well-handled and provide a fictional escape hatch for his literary alter ego, but his excursions into the recesses of the novelist's inner workroom provoke dismay at the airlessness of the working conditions and the joylessness of literary creation at even his rarefied level.

Don DeLillo typically provides the exhilarating nadir of literary joylessness in the figure of Bill Gray, the reclusive writer at the center of his last novel, *Mao II*. Combining the mania for privacy and the literary fastidiousness of J. D. Salinger and Thomas Pynchon, Bill Gray lives in solitude somewhere in upstate New York; his long recusancy from the scene has, naturally, made him a celebrity and the longer he lays low the more famous he becomes. "When a writer doesn't show his face he becomes a local symptom of God's famous reluctance to appear," he explains to a photographer who has come to take the first photographs of him in thirty years. Gray's literary anhedonia and obsessive reworking of his long-awaited novel make Powers's plaints read like "The Ode to Joy":

He looked at the sentence, six disconsolate words, and saw the entire book as it took occasional shape in his mind, a neutered near-human dragging through the house, humpbacked, hydrocephalic, with puckered lips and soft skin, dribbling brain fluid from its mouth. Took him all these years to realize this book was his hated adversary. Locked together in the forbidden room, had him in a chokehold.

However, DeLillo also manages to lend a public dimension to the writer's private paralysis and sense of ineffectuality. As Bill Gray muses to the photographer:

"There is a curious knot that binds novelists and terrorists. In the West we become famous effigies as our books lose the power to shape and influence. . . . Years ago I used to think it was possible for a novelist to alter the inner life of the culture. Now bomb-makers and gunmen have taken that territory. They make raids on human consciousness. What writers used to do before we were all incorporated."

The novel demonstrates this insight graphically in Bill Gray's quixotic and ultimately fatal foray into public life, a desperate attempt to harness his peculiar fame to the task of freeing a hostage in Beirut. The future, Gray and his creator intuit, belongs to crowds and those who can harness their angry energies—certainly not to the isolated and autonomous creative intelligence, which, for all the celebrity it may be proffered, remains powerless to alter the fundamental terms of the culture.

What is going on here? Why, at this particular juncture of our cultural history, have some of our most sophisticated novelists chosen to demystify their vocation and disillusion their audience? If you live to read and read to live, a literal apprehension of the literary portraits in these four novels will make you wonder whether art could ever really be worth such internal devastation—and whether such damaged souls should be trusted as guides to right thought and action.

Behind such questions lie a whole host of conundrums concerning tellers and tales, and the literary pathography industry hums along inexorably, manufacturing such conundrums for public consumption at an alarming rate. Still, what a startling shift in emphasis in the mythology of authorship from my own book-soaked sixties adolescence. In that era writer figures strutted through novels cockily, priapically (they were all males, of course), rebelliously. Samson Shillitoe, the poet–hero of Elliott Baker's 1964 novel *A Fine Madness,* can stand in for a whole corps of literary poster boys—a rugged epic poet in rampant revolt, laying intellectual waste to the psychiatrists' timid theories of adjustment and creativity and sexual waste to their wives. (Played in the film version, naturally, by Sean Connery.) In fact, a whole mystique of sexual potency gathered about the novelist, cultivated by writers from Henry Miller to Norman Mailer; penmanship and cocksmanship clearly went hand in hand. On the public stage as well, novelists cut impressive figures: here was Norman Mailer again (and again . . .), marching on the Pentagon, running for public office, sparring with José Torres (well, stabbing his wife too)—an avatar of an overreaching age. And here was Ken Kesey, a true cultural superhero, who wrote two of the finest novels of his generation only to move beyond the printed page to blaze a Day-Glo trail into the zeitgeist with his druggy Magic Bus odyssey. No flop sweat here, nor on more private figures like Richard Fariña, Kurt Vonnegut, Richard Brautigan, and Tom Robbins, whose antic novels communicated not just words but comprehensive attitudes to my generation. Writers *mattered.*

I speak of a time, of course, in a great swivet over conformity, inauthenticity, and sterility, for which the elixirs of literary creation were thought to be antidotes. Today writers are more commonly seen as providers of "content" for the multimedia assembly lines of the contemporary Grubway. But writers' confident assertions of cultural authority drew on a reservoir of trust built up over many, many decades, even centuries. The giants of modern American literature—Steinbeck, Hemingway, Faulkner, Eliot, Wharton, et al.—were living memories and their work had literally helped to define our national identity. These writers projected a mystique so powerful that people used it as template for their own self-definition. And many of the giants of European literature still trod the earth—and in some cases could be encountered personally. Susan Sontag wrote a while back in the *New Yorker* of being a book-drunk teenaged intellectual in Los Angeles and getting up the courage to make a cold call with a friend on Thomas Mann in Pacific Palisades. The heir to Goethe and the German humanistic tradition received these awestruck kids politely, if remotely, gave them a cup of tea, chatted with them, and sent them on their way. It felt like magic to Sontag and it feels like magic still. What figure might serve as a Thomas Mann equivalent today—assuming you could find a young Susan Sontag equivalent?

Before we succumb to the temptation, though, to unreel an invidious procession of mighty literary figures parading across the centuries, a look backward at the actual difficult circumstances of literary production in eras past would be salutary. No better corrective may be found than George Gissing's *New Grub Street*, the *The Information* of its day (Amis had to have had it in mind) and still a startlingly pertinent picture of the literary life. Precisely because of Gissing's mildly pedestrian Victorian realism, the absence of a Dickensian genius to transform character into archetype, the book has the air of complete veracity about writing and publishing circa 1882.

In outline and conception *New Grub Street* reads like a geometric proof of the axiom that in the literary world the innocent, the idealist, and the artist are fated to fall while the sharper, the opportunist, and the poseur will rise. Conspicuous in the first category is the book's hero-victim Edward Reardon, a novelist of high intent and meager income, whose gifts of invention, while real, are utterly unsuited to the incident-heavy manufacture of the three-decker novels required by the circulating libraries of the day ("he was trying to devise a 'plot,' the kind of literary Jack-in-the-box which might excite interest in the mass of readers, and this was alien to the natural working of his imagination"). Saddled with an unforgiving wife who demands he provide them with an adequate social position, poor Reardon cudgels his brain daily at his desk to the twin chiming of the bells of the Marylebone parish church and the adjoining workhouse—destinations all too plausible to him. Even more poignant, perhaps, is his novelist friend Biffen, who labors long in Flaubertian style ("Each sentence was as good as he could make it, harmonious to the ear") and grim poverty on his domestic epic of the everyday, *Mr. Bailey, Grocer* ("Shall I hint that it deals with the ignobly decent?"). Biffen's reward for his monklike integrity is predictable: devastatingly condescending reviews with lectures that "the first duty of a novelist is to tell a story," privation that leads to near-starvation, and finally a loneliness whose end is suicide.

Meanwhile, the path to the sunny uplands of well-padded prosperity is open to such as Jasper Milvain, the book's arch-literary operative and consummate trimmer. Given to such smug pronouncements as "Literature today is a trade . . . your successful man of letters is your skillful tradesman.

He thinks first and foremost of the markets" and "Many a fellow could write more in quantity, but they couldn't command my market. It's rubbish, but rubbish of a special quality," Jasper has all the angles figured and is completely without shame. So naturally he ends up marrying Reardon's widow and winning a coveted editorship. Then there is the cheerfully empty-headed Whelpdale, who enters the book as a proto-literary agent offering advice to aspirants for a fee and "recommending" their work to publishers. "Now that's one of the finest jokes I ever heard. A man who can't get anyone to publish his own books makes a living by telling other people how to write!" Milvain exclaims, anticipating by a century the creative writing industry. By book's end Whelpdale is prosperously editing *Chit-Chat,* a paper not unlike *USA Today,* addressing itself to the vast emerging audience of "the quarter educated" with articles no longer than two inches and full of "the lightest and frothiest of chit-chatty information," designed for swift digestion on trains and trams.

Enter the mass media, stage left. *New Grub Street* was conceived in a time not unlike our own when an explosion of mass communications had fundamentally altered the literary equation. On New Grub Street the hazards facing those unwilling to adapt were relatively straightforward: poverty, starvation, death. On Neo-Grub Street or the Grubway, as we have seen, baroque forms of demoralization or grotesque forms of adaptation seem to be the choices offered. No wonder some of our best novelists are blowing the lid off the postmodern literary dodge. And editors too: Michael Korda's amusingly chilling memoir of his time served as Jacqueline Susann's editor contains this tidbit: "When we had expressed anxiety about the unwritten manuscript, Irving [Mansfield, her husband and agent] told us it was Jackie (and the example of *Valley of the Dolls,* then approaching ten million copies sold) that he was selling and not as he put it indignantly, 'a goddamn pile of paper.' " Some would say we live in a post-Jacqueline Susann universe.

Authors share with presidents today the impossible conditions of office: it is hellishly difficult to inspire and lead either politically or spiritually when you are required to expose yourself utterly, to make your life, no pun intended, an open book. Leadership and pseudo-intimacy are in fundamental conflict. And the roles of president and novelist also have this in common: declining sway and public respect.

Of course, my search for spiritual guidance in the field of literature is a quaint anachronism. There is no shortage of claimants to the big job of resolving the spiritual confusions of the age in your local superstore—they just aren't found in the literature section anymore. Sub-Gwyn Barry productions like *The Celestine Prophecy, Mutant Message Down Under,* and *Embraced by the Light,* mega-sellers all, purport to bring their credulous readers succor and solace—news that there is a way and these pilgrim scribes have found it. These books tend to be self-published at first, and indeed their grandiose semiliteracy will be familiar to anyone who has done time in a publisher's slushpile. Amis has their number: "It wasn't bad literature. It was anti-literature. Propaganda aimed at the self. . . . They were like tragic babies; they were like pornography. They shouldn't be looked at. They really shouldn't be looked at." Well, they are looked at, by the millions, and publishers are rushing to fill the newly discovered meaning gap with a barrage of titles about finding God or something like Him or Her while riding a Harley or snowboarding the Himalayas. As one publisher put it in the *New York Times,* "We're living in a spiritual age, aren't we?"

All of which only further fuels the despair of the serious novelist, whose task it is not to dumb down the reader's sense of life and fate into a set of slogans and self-help propositions, but to deepen and complicate it. In a fine critique of minimalist fiction a few years back, the novelist Madison Smartt Bell made the lovely assertion that "If our lives do in fact lack variety and meaning, then maybe we had better make haste to invent some." But today's novelists know that the meanings they might discover or invent for our fragmented, improvisatory lives are tentative, less than universal, subject to revision at the turn of the cultural wheel—and almost certain to be drowned out by the ersatz "wisdom" in plentiful and profitable supply. Hence the comic despair with which some writers preemptively eviscerate the mystique of their calling. Hence the cold-eyed Milvainian calculation with which others play the career game.

In *If on a winter's night a traveler* Italo Calvino beautifully captures the mysterious way a mere book can hold sway over our imagination, compel our allegiance and faith. His book editor alter ego Cavedagna is intimate with all the mechanics of bookmaking, all the crotchets of authors. Knowing all he knows,

the true books for him remain others, those of the time when for him they were like messages from other worlds . . . and yet the true authors remain those who for him were only a name on a jacket, a word that was part of the title, authors who had the same reality as their characters, as the places mentioned in the books, who existed and didn't exist at the same time, like those characters and those countries. The author was an invisible point from which the books came, a void traveled by ghosts, an underground tunnel that put other worlds in communication with the chicken coop of his boyhood. . . .

As we slouch towards the Grubnet, a digital cyberspace in which books and authors alike will become dematerialized, available on demand twenty-four hours a day, that otherworldly innocence and mysterious remoteness that gave books their authority and that Cavedagna mourns become impossible to recapture—as distant and hard to imagine a state of mind as trusting a politician. We are all of us, readers and writers alike, exiles from the garden of innocent reading. Who knows what beasts await us in the new cultural wilderness?

Rupture, Verge, and Precipice
Precipice, Verge, and Hurt Not

Carole Maso

> Be not afraid. The isle is full of noises,
> Sounds and sweet airs that give delight and hurt not.
> —William Shakespeare

YOU ARE AFRAID. You are afraid, as usual, that the novel is dying. You think you know what a novel is: it's the kind you write. You fear you are dying.

You wonder where the hero went.

You wonder how things could have gotten so out of hand.

You ask where is one sympathetic, believable character?

You ask where is the plot?

You wonder where on earth is the conflict? The resolution? The dénouement?

You imagine yourself to be the holder of some last truth. You imagine yourself to be in some sinking, noble, gilt-covered cradle of civilization.

You romanticize your fin de siècle, imbuing it with meaning, overtones, implications.

You are still worried about TV.

You are still worried about the anxiety of influence.

You say there will be no readers in the future, that there are hardly any readers now. You count your measly 15,000—but you have always underestimated everything.

You say language will lose its charms, its ability to charm, its power to mesmerize.

You say the world turns, spins away, or that we turn from it. You're pretty desolate.

You mutter a number of the usual things. You say " . . . are rust," " . . . are void," " . . . are torn."

You think you know what a book is, what reading is, what constitutes a literary experience. In fact you've been happy all these years to legislate the literary experience. All too happy to write the rules.

You think you know what the writer does, what the reader does. You're pretty smug about it.

You think you know what the reader wants: a good old-fashioned story.

You think you know what a woman wants: a good old-fashioned—

You find me obnoxious, uppity. You try to dismiss me as hysterical or reactionary or out of touch because I won't enter that cozy little pact with you anymore. Happy little subservient typing "my" novel, the one you've been dictating all these years.

You rely on me to be dependent on you for favors, publication, $$$$$$$$, canonization.

You are afraid. Too smug in your middle ground with your middlebrow. Everything threatens you.

You say music was better then: the Rolling Stones, the Who, the Beatles, Fleetwood Mac. You're boring me.

You say hypertext will kill print fiction. You pit one against the other in the most cynical and transparent ways in hopes we'll tear each other to bits

While you watch. You like to watch. Hold us all in your gaze.

Just as you try to pit writing against theory, prose against poetry, film against video, etc., as you try to hold on to your little piece of the disappearing world.

But I, for one, am on to you. Your taste for blood, your love of competition, your need to feel endangered, beleaguered, superior. Your need to reiterate, to reassert your power, your privilege, because it erodes.

Let's face it, you're panicked.

You think an essay should have a hypothesis, a conclusion, should argue points. You really do bore me.

You'd like to put miraculous, glowing glyphs on a screen on one side and modest ink on pretty white paper on the other. You set up, over and over, false dichotomies. Easy targets. You reduce almost everything, as I reduce you now. Tell me, how does it feel?

You're real worried. You say sex will be virtual. The casting couch, virtual. But you know as well as I do that all the other will continue, you betcha, so why are you so worried?

You fear your favorite positions are endangered. Will become obsolete.

You believe you have more to lose than other people in other times.

You romanticize the good old days—the record skipping those nights long ago while you were making love, while you were having real sex with—

Hey, was that me? The Rolling Stones crooning: "I see a red door and I want it painted black, painted black, painted black. . . ."

Want it painted black.

Or: "Brown Sugar, how come you dance so good, dance so good, dance so good . . . ???"

You want to conserve everything. You worship false prophets. You're sick over your (dwindling) reputation.

You're so cavalier, offering your hand. . . .

Jenny Holzer: "The future is stupid."

I remember the poet-dinosaurs that evening at the dinner table munching on their leafy greens, going extinct even as they spoke, whispering "language poetry" (that was the evil that night), shuddering.

You fear the electronic ladyland. Want it painted black.

You're afraid of junk food. The real junk food and the metaphoric junk food the media feeds you. Want it painted black . . .

painted black.

You fear the stylist (as you have defined style) will perish.

You consider certain art forms to be debased and believe that in the future all true artists will disappear. Why do you believe other forms to be inferior to your own?

You consider certain ways of thinking about literature to be debased. You can't decide whether they're too rigorous or too reckless, or both.

Edmund Wilson, Alfred Kazin, Harold Bloom *et fils*—make my day.

You think me unladylike. Hysterical. Maybe crazy. Unreadable. You put me in your unreadable box where I am safe. Where I am quiet. More lady-like.

In your disdainful box labeled "experimental." Labeled "do not open." Labeled "do not review."

You see a red door and you want it painted black.

No more monoliths.

You who said "hegemony" and "domino theory" and "peace with honor."

All the deaths for nothing. All the dark roads you've led us down. No more.

The future: where we're braced always for the next unspeakably monstrous way to die—or to kill.

All the dark deserted roads you've led me down, grabbing at my breasts, tearing at my shirt, my waistband: first date.

Second date: This is how to write a book.

Third date: Good girl! Let's publish it!!!

Brown Sugar, how come you dance so good?

Fourth date: Will you marry me?

You fear the future, OK. You fear anything new. Anything that disrupts your sense of security and self. Everything threatens you.

Where is the change over the course of the thing in the hero?

Where is the hero?

Where's the conflict? Where the hell is the dénouement?

I see your point. But haven't you asked us to write your fiction for just a little too long now? Couldn't we—

Couldn't we, maybe just possibly, coexist?

Why does my existence threaten yours?

It's been too long now that you've asked me to be you. Insisted I be you.

Lighten up. Don't be so afraid. Put up your hand. Say: Bunny, Alfred, Harold, bye-bye.

You fear. You fear the television. You loathe and adore the television.

You feel numbed and buzzed by so much electronics. Numbed and buzzed by so much future.

I'm getting a little tired of this "you" and "I." Still I am learning a few new things about you—and about me.

The future of literature. The death of the novel. You love, for some reason, the large, glitzy questions and statements. And now we've all been gathered here, in this nice journal, to write on the assigned topic. But the question bores me—and all the usual ways of thinking and speaking and writing anymore.

I'm sorry you are so afraid. You want it to be something like the movie *2001,* the future. You want it to be ludicrous, the future, easily dismissable. Like me. If only I didn't dance so good. You demand to know, How come

you dance so good, dance so good, dance so good . . . ???

You can't see a place for yourself in it and it frightens you. You dig in your heels as a result. Spend all your considerable intelligence and energy conserving, preserving, holding court, posturing, tenaciously holding on, now as you munch your last green leaves, yum.

Where is the resolution of the conflict? Where the fuck is the conflict?

What if a book might also include, might also be, the tentative, the hesitant, the doubt you most fear and despise?

Lyn Hejinian: "Closure is misanthropic."

Fear of growth, fear of change, fear of breaking one's own mold, fear of disturbing the product, fear of ridicule, fear of indifference, fear of failure, fear of invisibility, fear of, fear of, fear of. . . .

You say that language will cease to be respected, will no longer move us. But we're already becoming numb thanks to what you are afraid to give up. What you flood the market with.

Soyinka: "I am concerned about preserving a special level of communication, a level very different from Oprah Winfrey."

Wish: That all Oprah Winfrey fiction be put to bed now. Its fake psychologies, its "realisms." Its pathetic 2 plus 2.

Language of course has an enormous capacity to lie, to make false shapes, to be glib, to make common widgets, three parts this and two parts that.

Wish: That all the fiction of lies be put to bed.

That the dishonesty running rampant through much contemporary fiction be recognized as such.

What deal must I strike in order to be published by you? What pose, bargain, stance, is it I must strike with you now?

What mold do you make of me to pour your elixir, your fluid into, and then reward?

The bunny mold? The kitten mold? The flower mold? The damaged flower mold? Pregnant at twelve, illiterate, but with a twist? The gay mold? The white trash mold? The battered child mold? The bad girl mold?

Paint me black. Paint me Latina. Paint me Native American. Paint me Asian and then pour me into your mold. Use me. Co-opt me. Market me.

Debase me and in the future I shall rise anew out of your cynicism and scorn—smiling, lovely, free.

I know a place that burns brighter than a million suns.

Wish list: That the business people who have taken over the publishing houses will focus themselves elsewhere and leave the arts alone again.

Not to own or colonize or dominate. . . .

Despite all efforts to tame it, manage it, control it, outsmart it, language resists your best efforts; language is still a bunch of sturdy, glittering charms in the astonished hand.

A utopia of possibility. A utopia of choice.

And I am huddled around the fire of the alphabet, still.

Even though you say one word next to the other will cease to be cherished.

You say rap music is poison. Hypertext is poison. You want it painted black.

Even though you call me sentimental—on the one hand girly-girl, on the other hand loud-mouthed bitch, on the one hand interesting and talented writer, on the other hand utterly out-of-touch idealist, romantic—it is you who wants the nineteenth century back again. When things were dandy for you, swell. You want to believe in the old coordinates, the old shapes. To believe in whatever it was you believed in then. You were one of the guys who dictated the story, sure, I remember. Who made up the story and now go teaching it all over the place. But even then, when you sat around making it up, even then, my friend, it had nothing to do with me. With my world. With what I saw and how I felt.

Wish: That all graduate writing programs with their terminal degrees, stop promoting such tiresome recipes for success or go (financially) bankrupt.

Your false crescendos. Climaxes. False for me, at any rate.

The future is all the people who've ever been kept out, singing.

In the future everything will be allowed.

So the future is for you, too. Not to worry. *But not only for you.*

For you, but not only for you.

Not to discard the canon, but to enlarge it.

No more monoliths. No more Mick Jaggers. No more O. J. Simpsons. No more James Joyces. No more heroes.

Everything threatens you. Hacks, hackers, slacks, slackers, cybergirls with their cybercurls and wiles, poets of every sort. Rock bands with girls.

You believe your (disappearing) time represents some last golden age of enlightenment, to be guarded, protected, reproduced against the approaching mindlessness, depravity, electronic states of America.

But maybe as you become more and more threatened, you'll take a few more risks yourself. Who knows? Anything is possible in the future.

Wish list: That the homogeneity end. That the mainstream come to acknowledge, for starters, the thousand refracted, disparate beauties out there.

That the writers and the readers stop being treated by the mainstream houses like idiot children. That the business people get out and stop imposing their "taste" on everyone.

Wish: That as writers we be aware of our own desire to incorporate, even unconsciously, the demands and anxieties of publishers and reject them, the demands and anxieties of the marketplace.

That the business people go elsewhere.

Market me. Promote me. Sanitize me. Co-opt me. Plagiarize me. Market me harder.

Wish list: That the grade inflation for a certain kind of writing stop, and that the middlebrow writers assume their middle position so that everyone else might finally have a place too. Be considered seriously too. Be read, too.

Paint me black. Paint me Latina. Paint me Chinese. Pour me into your mold and sell me harder.

Fuck me (over) harder.

Those of us jockeying for position in the heavens, intent on forever, major reputations, major motion pictures and $$$$$$$$, life after life after life after death, forget about it.

Wish: That straight white males consider the impulse to cover the entire world with their words, fill up every page, every surface, everywhere.

Thousand-page novels, tens and tens of vollmanns—I mean volumes.

Not to own or colonize or dominate anymore.

"Well we've been kept from ourselves too long, don't you think?" an old woman in Central Park says to a friend.

Two women in the park at dusk.

Turn the beat around:

The pauses and rhythms and allowances of Laurie Anderson. The glow of Jenny Holzer. The ranting and passion of Courtney Love. Brilliance of Susan Howe. Brilliance of Erin Mouré. Theresa Cha. Visionary P. J. Harvey.

The future is feminine, for real, this time.

The future is Emily Dickinson and Emily Brontë and Gertrude Stein still. The future is still Maya Deren and Billie Holiday.

Language is a rose and the future is still a rose opening.

It is beautiful there in the future. Irreverent, wild.

The future is women, for real this time. I'm sorry, but it's time you got used to it.

Reading on a train by the light the river gives. The woman next to me asleep. Two plastic bags at her feet. Lulling, lovely world. And I am witness to it all—that slumber—and then her awakening—so vulnerable, sensation streaming back, the world returned, the river and the light the river gives, returning language, touch, and smell. The world retrieved. I am privileged to be next to her as she moves gracefully from one state to the next, smiling slightly. I recognize her delight. It is taken away, and it is given back. The miracle and mystery of this life in one middle-aged black woman on the Metro North next to me. The Hudson River widening.

Let all of this be part of the story too. A woman dreaming next to water.

The future: all the dreams we've been kept from. All the things yet to dream.

An opening of possibility. A land of a thousand dances.

I want sex and hypersex and cybersex, why not?

The river mysteriously widening, as she opens her eyes.

We can say, if we like, that the future will be plural.

Our voices processed through many systems—or none at all.

A place where a thousand birds are singing.

"The isle is full of noises . . ."

A place without the usual dichotomies. No phony divisions between mind and body, intelligence and passion, nature and technology, private and public, within and without, male and female.

May we begin a dialogue there in the future. May we learn something from each other. Electronic writing will help us to think about impermanence, facility, fragility and freedom, spatial intensities, irreverences, experimentation, new worlds, clean slates. Print writing will allow us new respect for the mark on the page, the human hand, the erasure, the hesitation, the mistake.

Electronic writing will give us a deeper understanding of the instability of texts, of worlds.

Print writing will remind us of our love for the physical, for the sensual world. And for the light only a book held in one's hands can give. The book taken to bed or the beach—the words dancing with the heat and the sea—and the mouth now suddenly on my salty neck.

Electronic writing shall inspire magic. Print writing shall inspire magic. Ways to heal:

"Intoxicated with Serbian nationalist propaganda, one charge is that X took part in the murder of a Muslim civilian, F, by forcing another Muslim to bite off F's testicles."

What is a book and how might it be reimagined, opened up, transformed to accommodate all we've seen, all we've been hurt by, all that's been given, all that's been taken away:

" . . . deliberately infecting subjects with fatal diseases, killing 275,000 of the elderly, the deformed and other 'useless eaters' through the guise of euthanasia, and killing 112 Jews simply to fill out a university skeleton collection."

No more monoliths. No more gods.

"Let us go then, you and I. . . ."

No more sheepish, mindless devotion. No more quiet supplication.

All the dark roads you've led us down no more.

You will call me naive, childlike, irreverent, idealistic, offensive, outrageous, defiant at times, because I do not believe in a literature of limitation, in a future of limitation. I annoy you with this kind of talk, I know. You've told me many times before. You'd like me to step into my quiet box. You're so cavalier, as you offer your hand.

It sure looks like prose, but it's poetry. It sure seems to be poetry, but I think it's a novel. It just looks like a mess, really, a lot of ranting and raving and discontinuous sad and happy stuff—but it's an essay—about the future.

The future. Possibility will reign. My students poised on some new threshold. We're too diversified, we're too fractured, all too close in proximity suddenly—one world.

One wild world,

Free of categories, free of denominations, dance and fiction and performance and installation and video and poetry and painting—one world—every hyper- and cyber-

And in upstate New York a woman sees fields of flax and iris and cattails and dreams of making paper. And dreams of creating an Art Farm—a place just for experimenting with unusual indigenous fibers, a real space for bookbinding, an archive, a library, a gallery.

Dream: That this new tolerance might set a tone, give example. This openness in acceptance of texts, of forms, this freedom, this embrace will serve as models for how to live. Will be the model for a new world order—in my dream. A way to live together better—in my dream.

Godard: "A film like this, it's a bit as if I wanted to write a sociological essay in the form of a novel, and all I had to do it with was notes of music. Is that what cinema is? And am I right to continue doing it?"

But I do believe, and no doubt childishly, unquestioningly, in the supremacy of beauty, in pattern, in language, as a child believes in language, in diversity, in the possibility of justice—even after everything we have seen—in the impulse to speak—even after everything.

"Peder Davis, a bouncy, tow-headed 5-year-old, shook his head and said, 'I would tell him: You shoot down this building? You put it back together.

And I would say, You redo those people.'"

One hundred and sixty-eight dead in Oklahoma bombing.

"Peder said he drew 'a house with eyes that was blue on the sides.' He explained, 'It was the building that exploded, in heaven.'"

Wish: That writing again, through its audacity, generosity, possibility, irreverence, wildness, teach us how to better live.

The world doesn't end.

The smell of the air. The feel of the wind in late April.

You can't have a genuine experience of nature except in nature. You can't have a genuine experience of language except in language. And for those of us for whom language is the central drama, the captivating, imaginative, open, flexible act, there can never be a substitute or a replacement.

Language continually opening new places in me.

A picture of a bird will never be a bird. And a bird will never be a picture of a bird. So relax.

The world doesn't end, my friend. So stop your doomsday song. Or Matthew Arnold: "The end is everywhere: Art still has truth, take refuge there."

All will perish, but not this: language opening like a rose.

And many times I have despaired over the limits of language, the recalcitrance of words that refuse to yield, won't glimmer, won't work anymore. All the outmoded forms. Yet I know it is part of it, I know that now; it's part of the essential mystery of the medium—and that all of us who are in this thing for real have to face this, address this, love this, even.

The struggles with shape, with silence, with complacency. The impossibility of the task.

You say destined to perish, death of the novel, end of fiction, over and over.

But Matthew Arnold, on the cusp of another century, dreams: art.

And I say faced with the eternal mysteries, one, if so inclined, will make fictive shapes.

What it was like to be here. To hold your hand.

An ancient impulse, after all.

As we reach, trying to recapture an original happiness, pleasure, peace—

Reaching—

The needs that language mirrors and engenders and satisfies are not going away. And are not replaceable.

The body with its cellular alphabet. And, in another alphabet, the desire to get that body onto the page.

There will be works of female sexuality, finally.

Feminine shapes.

All sorts of new shapes. Language, a rose, opening.

It's greater than we are, than we'll ever be. That's why I love it. Kneeling at the altar of the impossible. The self put back in its proper place.

The miracle of language. The challenge and magic of language.

Different than the old magic. I remember you liked to saw women in half and put them back together, once. Configure them in ways most pleasing to you.

You tried once to make language conform. Obey. You tried to tame it. You tried to make it sit, heel, jump through hoops.

You like to say I am reckless. You like to say I lack discipline. You say my work lacks structure. I've heard it a hundred times from you. But nothing could be farther from the truth.

In spite of everything, my refusal to hate you, to take you all that seriously, to be condescended to—

Still, too often I have worried about worldly things. Too often have I worried about publishing, about my so-called career, fretted over the so-so writers who are routinely acclaimed, rewarded, given biscuits and other treats— this too small prison of self where I sometimes dwell.

Too often I have let the creeps upset me.

The danger of the sky.

The danger of April.

If you say language is dying. . . .

Susan Howe: "Poetry is redemption from pessimism."

April in the country. Already so much green. So much life. So much. Even with half the trees still bare. Poking up through the slowly warming earth, the tender shoots of asparagus. Crocus. Bloodroot.

This vulnerable and breakable heart.

As we dare to utter something, to commit ourselves, to make a mark on a page or a field of light.

To incorporate this dangerous and fragile world. All its beauty. All its pain.

You who said "hegemony" and "domino theory" and "peace with honor."

To not only tolerate but welcome work that is other than the kind we do.

To incorporate the ache of Vietnam, the mistake of it, incapable of being erased or changed. To invent forms that might let that wound stand—

If we've learned anything, yet.

Summer 1885

Brother and Sister's Friend—
    "Sweet Land of Liberty" is a superfluous Carol till it concerns ourselves—then it outrealms the Birds . . .
    Your Hollyhocks endow the House, making Art's inner Summer, never Treason to Nature's. Nature will be closing her Picnic when you return to America, but you will ride Home by sunset, which is far better.
    I am glad you cherish the Sea. We correspond, though I never met him.
    I write in the midst of Sweet-Peas and by the side of Orioles, and could put my hand on a Butterfly, only he withdraws.
    Touch Shakespeare for me.

"Be not afraid. The isle is full of noises, Sounds and sweet airs that give delight and hurt not."

Fifty years now since World War II. She sits in the corner and weeps.

And hurt not.

Six million dead.

"Well, we've been kept from ourselves long enough, don't you think?"

We dare to speak. Trembling, and on the verge.

Extraordinary things have been written. Extraordinary things will continue to be written.

Nineteen ninety-five: Vinyl makes its small comeback. To the teenage music freak, to the classical music fiend and to the opera queen, CDs are now being disparaged as producing too cold, too sanitary a sound. Vinyl is being sought out again for its warmer, richer quality.

Wish: That we be open-minded and generous. That we fear not.

That the electronic page understand its powers and its limitations. Nothing replaces the giddiness one feels at the potential of hypertext. Entirely new shapes might be created, different ways of thinking, of perceiving.

Kevin Kelly, executive director of *Wired* magazine: "The first thing discovered by Jaron Lanier [the virtual reality pioneer] is to say what is reality? We get to ask the great questions of all time: What is life? What is human? What is civilization? And you ask it not in the way the old philosophers asked it, sitting in armchairs, but by actually trying it. Let's try and *make* life. Let's try and *make* community."

And now the Extropians, who say they can achieve immortality by downloading the contents of the human brain onto a hard disk. . . .

So turn to the students. Young visionaries. Who click on the Internet, the cyberworld in their sleep. Alvin Lu: citizen of the universe, the whole world at his fingertips. In love with the blinding light out there, the possibility, world without end, his love of all that is the future.

Let the fictions change shape, grow, accommodate. Let the medium change if it must; the artist persists.

You say all is doomed, but I say Julio Cortázar. I say Samuel Beckett. I say Marcel Proust. Virginia Woolf. I say García Lorca and Walt Whitman. I say Mallarmé. I say Ingeborg Bachmann. *The Apu Trilogy* will lie next to *Hamlet. Vivre sa vie* will live next to *Texts for Nothing*.

These fragmented prayers.

Making love around the fire of the alphabet.

Wish: That we not hurt each other purposely anymore.

A literature of love. A literature of tolerance. A literature of difference.

Saving the best of what was good in the old. Not to discard indiscriminately, but not to hold on too tightly either. To go forward together, unthreatened for once.

The future is Robert Wilson and JLG. The future is Martha Graham, still. The vocabularies of dance, of film, of performance.

The disintegration of categories.

If you say that language is dying, then what do you know of language?

I am getting a little tired of this you-and-I bit. But it tells me one important thing: *that I do not want it to have to be this way.* I do not believe it has to continue this way—you over there alternately blustery and cowering, me over here, defensive, angry.

Wish: A sky that is not divided. A way to look at the screen of the sky with its grandeur, its weather, its color, its patterns of bird flight, its airplanes and accidents and poisons, its mushroom clouds.

Its goldfinches frescoed against an aqua-blue dome.

Wish: That the sky go on forever. That we stop killing each other. That we allow each other to live.

April 1995 in New York City and the long-awaited Satyajit Ray Festival begins. For years he's been kept from us. Who decides, finally, what is seen, what is read, and why? And how much else has been deleted, omitted, neglected, ignored, buried, treated with utter indifference or contempt.

And in conversation with the man, my friend, a famous poet in fact, and the topic moved to someone we both knew who had just been operated on; and he said "masectomy," and I said back, "Yes, a mastectomy, a mastectomy," and he said "masectomy" like "vasectomy," and I said only under my breath, "It's mas*tec*tomy, idiot," ashamed, embarrassed and a little intimidated, that was the worst part, a little unsure. That it made me question what I of course knew, that was the worst part—because of his easy confidence saying "masectomy," his arrogance, he hadn't even bothered to learn the right word, a *poet*, for God's sake, a man who worked with words, who should have known the right word for the removal of a breast, don't you think?

Mastectomy.

The undeniable danger of the sky.

Adrienne Rich: "Poetry means refusing the choice to kill or die."

Wish: That the straight white male give in just a little more gracefully. Call in its Michael Douglases, its suspect Hollywood, its hurt feelings, its fear— move over some.

After your thousands of years of affirmative action, give someone else a chance—just a chance.

The wish is for gentleness. The wish is for allowances.

"What is the phrase for the moon? And the phrase for love? By what name are we to call death? I do not know. I need a little language such as lovers use. . . ."

Wish: That the typical *New Yorker* story become the artifact it is and assume its proper place in the artifact museum, and not be mistaken for something still alive. Well we've just about had it with all the phony baloney, don't you think?

That the short story and the novel as they evolve and assume new, utterly original shapes might be treated gently. And with optimism. That is the wish.

That hypertext and all electronic writing still in its infancy be treated with something other than your fear and your contempt.

That, poised on the next century, we fear not. Make no grand pronouncements.

You say that language is dying, will die.

And at times I have felt for you, even loved you. But I have never believed you.

The Ebola virus is now. The Hanta virus. HIV. And that old standby, malaria. Live while you can. Tonight, who knows, may be our last. We may not even make the millennium, so don't worry about it so much.

All my friends who have died holding language in their throats, into the end. All my dead friends.

Cybernauts return from time to time wanting to see a smile instead of a colon followed by a closed parenthesis—the online sign for a smile. When someone laughs out loud they want to hear real laughter in the real air, not just the letters L.O.L. in front of them. Ah, yes. World while there is world.

A real bird in the real sky and then perhaps a little prose poem or something in the real sky, or the page or the screen or the human heart, pulsing.

"I do not know which to prefer,
The beauty of inflections
Or the beauty of innuendoes.
The blackbird whistling
Or just after."

One world.

The future of literature is utopic. As surely as my friends Ed and Alan will come this weekend to visit bearing rose lentils. As long as one can say "rose," can say "lentil."

Gary dying, saying "Kappa maki."

You say, *over*. But I say, *no*.

I say faith and hope and trust and forever right next to wretched and hate and misery and hopeless.

In the future we will finally be allowed to live, just as we are, to imagine, to glow, to pulse.

Let the genres blur if they will. Let the genres redefine themselves.

Language is a woman, a rose constantly in the process of opening.

Vibrant, irresistible, incandescent.

Whosoever has allowed the villanelle to enter them or the sonnet. Whosoever has let in one genuine sentence, one paragraph, has felt that seduction like a golden thread being pulled slowly through one. . . .

Wish: That forms other than those you've invented or sanctioned through your thousands of years of privilege might arise and be celebrated.

"Put another way, it seems to me that we have to rediscover everything about everything. There is only one solution, and that is to turn one's back on American cinema. . . . Up until now we have lived in a closed world. Cinema fed on cinema, imitating itself. I now see that in my first films I did things because I had already seen them in the cinema. If I showed a police inspector drawing a revolver from his pocket, it wasn't because of the logic of the situation I wanted to describe demanded it, but because I had seen police inspectors in other films drawing revolvers at this precise moment and in this precise way. The same thing has happened in painting. There have been periods of organization and imitation and periods of rupture. We are now in a period of rupture. We must turn to life again. We must move into modern life with a virgin eye."

—Jean-Luc Godard, 1966

Wish: That Alvin Lu might wander in the astounding classroom of the world through time and space, endlessly inspired, endlessly enthralled by what he finds there. That he be allowed to reinvent freely, revel freely.

My professor once and now great friend, Barbara Page, out there too, ravenous, furious and without fear, inventing whole new worlds, ways of experiencing the text. New freedoms.

The world doesn't end, says Charles Simic. Engraved on our foreheads in ash, turned into a language of stars or birdsong across a vast sky; it stays. Literature doesn't end—but it may change shapes, be capable of things we cannot even imagine yet.

Woolf: "What is the phrase for the moon? And the phrase for love? By what name are we to call death? I do not know. I need a little language such as lovers use, words of one syllable such as children speak when they come into the room and find their mother sewing and pick up the scrap of bright wool, a feather, or a shred of chintz. I need a howl; a cry."

Charlotte Brontë: "My sister Emily loved the moors. Flowers brighter than the rose bloomed in the blackest of the heath for her; out of a sullen hollow in the livid hill-side her mind could make an Eden. She found in the bleak solitude many and dear delights; and not the least and best loved was—liberty."

The future will be gorgeous and reckless, and words, those luminous charms, will set us free again. If only for a moment.

Whosoever has allowed the language of lovers to enter them, the language of wound and pain and solitude and hope. Whosoever has dug in the miracle of the earth. Mesmerizing dirt, earth, word.

Allowed love in. Allowed despair in.

Words are the ginger candies my dying friends have sucked on. Or the salve of water.

Precious words, contoured by silence. Informed by the pressure of the end.

Words are the crow's-feet embedded in the skin of the father I love. Words are like that to me, still.

Words are the music of her hair on the pillow.

Words are the lines vibrating in the forest or in the painting. Pressures that enter us—bisect us, order us, disorder us, unite us, free us, help us, hurt us, cause anxiety, pleasure, pain.

Words are the footprints as they turn away in the snow.

There is no substitute for the language I love.

My father, one state away but still too far, asks over the telephone if I might take a photo of this bluebird, the first I have ever seen, because he hears how filled with delight I am by this fleeting sighting. But it's so tiny, it flies so fast, it's so hard to see. So far away. Me, with my small hunk of technology, pointing. With my nostalgia machine. My box that says fleeting, my box that says future,

My pleasure machine. My weeping machine that dreams: keep.

This novel that says desire and fleeting and unfinished.

Unfinished and left that way. Unfinished, not abandoned. Unfinished, not because of death or indifference or loss of faith, or nerve, just unfinished.

Not to draw false conclusions anymore. Not to set up false polarities. Unfinished and left that way, if necessary.

To allow everyone to write, to thrive, to live.

The Baltimore oriole returned from its American tropics at the edge of this frame now. I wait.

On this delicious precipice.

And nothing replaces this hand moving across the page, as it does now, intent on making a small mark and allowing it to stand on this longing surface.

Writing *oriole*. Imagining freedom. All that is possible.

April in the country. My hands in the dark earth, or the body of a woman, or an ordinary, gorgeous sentence.

Whosoever has let the hand linger on a burning thigh, or a shining river of light. . . .

Whosoever has allowed herself to be dazzled by the motion of the alphabet,

Or has let music into the body. Or has allowed music to fall onto the page.

Wish: To live and allow others to live. To sing and allow others to sing—while we can.

And hurt not.

Fleeting and longing moment on this earth. We were lucky to be here.

I close my eyes and hear the intricate chamber music of the world. An intimate, complicated, beautiful conversation in every language, in every tense, in every possible medium and form—incandescent.

—for Alvin, Barbara, and Judith
1 June 1995

Like the clarinet with the flute, like the French horn with the oboe, like the violin and the piano—take the melody from me, when it's time.

25 April 1995
Germantown, New York

A walk around the loop and I notice the bloodroot has begun to bloom. A bluebird, two bluebirds! the first I've ever seen, over by the convent. Before my eyes I see an infant clasping a small bird as depicted in Renaissance painting and sculpture. The world begins again. In this vision. In the words *bloodroot* and *bluebird*. And the goldfinches too are suddenly back. Today I saw three enormous turtles sunning themselves at a pond. The bliss of being on leave from teaching is beyond description. I recall Dickinson when someone mused that time must go very slowly for her, saying "Time! Why time was all I wanted!" And so ditto. Blissful time. Writing, walking every day. I am keeping depression at bay, mania in check. All private sufferings and hurt are somehow more manageable here in solitude. The moment seems all now. The imaginative event, the natural event (two wild turkeys in the woods), the sexual event, and the constantly changing and evolving forms in language for all of this. John sends a note to remind me that my essay is due for the *Review of Contemporary Fiction* on May 1, but that I may have a small extension. I should be finishing up *Defiance* but all I can think about are my erotic études—again feeling on the threshold of something amazing and out of reach. I'm extremely excited—hard to describe—my brain feels unhinged. . . .

I must make a note as to where to move the daffodils, the iris. The earth in my hands. A wand of forsythia like a light in my hands. I think of Barbara an hour away, the glowing glyphs coming off the screen in her study. The whole world—luminous, luminous. We were lucky to be here. Even in pain and uncertainty and rage and fear—some fear. In exhaustion.

Too much energy has gone into this Brown/Columbia decision. Where shall I end up? I have only partially succeeded in keeping it all in its proper place. I've had to work too hard to keep my mind at the proper distance. It takes its toll. I've needed the space to think, to dream other things. It hardly matters today though; another étude brews.

The *RCF* essay now in the back of my head. What to say? What can be said? How to use it to learn something, explore something I need to explore. When thinking of literature, the past and the present all too often infuriate me: everyone, everything that's been kept out. The future won't, can't be the same and yet . . . one worries it. What I wonder most is if there is a way, whether there might be a way in this whole wide world, to forgive them. Something for the sake of my own work, my own life I need to do—have needed to do a long time. Perhaps in my essay I will make an attempt, the first movement toward some sort of reconciliation, at any rate. If it's possible. To set up the drama that might make it possible.

This breakable heart.

April. How poised everything seems. How wonderfully ready. And I, too, trembling—and on the verge. . . .

Rivages Roses *for Niels Bohr*

Bradford Morrow

WE CONVENED, LATE summer, between the wars. My friends and I traveled by ferry and train, slept sitting chins on chests, to join the others at Como in the lake district. We came from all over the continent, from Munich and Brussels, from Budapest, Göttingen, from Vienna, Karlsruhe, Berlin, Copenhagen. It was a disturbing moment in the life of our science. No one had yet seen the center of an atom, but our masters, whom we revered, were working on ways to turn one inside out, thus to gaze at the soul of God, whom I always have thought of as a holy chaos of numbers through which—if we could but bring them into balance, summation, coherence— we could know our maker. Physics has always been for me a kind of faith, in other words. And this journey was a pilgrimage as much as anything else, to hear Niels Bohr attempt to reconcile the opposition of matter as wave and as particle, to harmonize the apparently conflicting views of classic physics and quantum theory.

He arrived from his Institute for Theoretical Physics on the edge of the Faelledpark, where he's been at work with Werner Heisenberg, the youthful father of the Uncertainty Principle. I hadn't ever seen him before this after-noon, but caught sight of him as he emerged from a car, and was struck by his warm fierce eyes and horselike head. Blunt wide lips, scissored hair. His suit was of a graybrown wool, simply cut, and shoes were well worn in long ago but shined bright as oil.

"Thank you," in a lilting Danish accent, to the *ragazzo* who carried his bags into the hotel. "Thank you," and followed him up the stone staircase.

As I watched them—Heisenberg followed, toting his own tatty valise—I knew that if I learned nothing else during my years studying at the Institute, I learned that a good part of theoretical physics is instinct. Any machine can be taught to play the scales. There was a Frenchman who, in the century past, built a mechanical duck, dressed it with feathers and a beak that would open and close after you fed it a berry. The duck could quack and waggle its tail. Having digested the berry, a gooseberry perhaps, it could even produce a pellet of excrement. No doubt, with adjustments and further hardware, this duck could be made to perform a Bach partita. Any closed system can be made to behave in pure, predictable ways. It is the true artist who by instinct draws inferences *between* notes. Neither the amateur nor the ma-chine cherishes silences, dynamics, nuance, the joy of an educated guess.

So it is with science. Bohr has the look of an intuitive virtuoso in those relentless eyes. Set any instrument before him—oboe, violin, a calliope—and leave him alone for an hour, and when you return I have no doubt he'd play it like a master.

And so we have come to hear him speak tomorrow afternoon. Nature is changing before our microcosmic eyes (not nature! but rather our eyes themselves, I should say) and little is making any sense to us now. Bohr may give us something to hold on to even as laws of Newton and Maxwell, laws we had always lived by, were no longer bearing up under the pressure of our new numbers and the findings we were seeing from our crude but precious instruments, our tungsten cylinders and slitted glass. Lord help us, Einstein himself seems now lost in the radiant blurry maze of a cosmos defined by uncertainty.

Even now, two generations later, I think of this man whom I never met, my mother's father's first cousin, Edward Hoffmann, and feel a terrible affinity with him, though none of our experiences could be considered remotely common. He died before I was born, for one. He lived in places I have yet to visit, possessed what I have been told was less an analytical than a physical mind, worked well in laboratory settings. More chemist than mathematician and—I would like to think—a hard worker who had his moments of radiance.

In our family of farmers and country doctors, his memory is preserved simultaneously as black sheep and tribal hero. To me he has always been a distant angel of sorts, and the few writings he saw into print—at least what I have been able to track down; there may be monographs I'll never find—I cannot claim to understand.

The great exception, and what brings Edward Hoffmann to mind just now, is that I share—these decades later and for reasons all my own, reasons he would probably understand no better than I understand the technologies of his craft—a fondness for the idea known as complementarity.

Late summer, warm. A walk after dinner. I looked for Bohr at the banquet but didn't see him among the others. Word is he's putting final touches on his address for tomorrow. The air here along the shores is heavy as pewter and as dark. Lights of the lakeside villas and hotels twinkle and shimmer, reflected on the water. I see a couple in a small boat out on the lake. The wake that tails their craft ridges the watery face of Como like iron filings drawn behind a magnetic charge. I wonder, Are they in love, their molecular hearts thrumming hard? Someone surely should be in love in such an evocative setting as this. Yes, I must believe that they are, and that the reason they are still out there, on the flat back of this mountain lake north of

Milan, is because they don't much want to row back to shore, where they will be forced to reenter the world, the other world.

We are between wars, as I say, because we are always between wars. Between great wars and many of us know it, although this occasion, which the awful Mussolini means for us to celebrate, has nothing to do with war per se.

A lake is not a lake, Bohr not Bohr. Love is not love but a noise that sounds nothing like love's odd noises. That much is known. And yet it is equally true that a lake is a lake, Bohr is Bohr, love is love. This is also known.

The contradictions between classical mechanistic physics and what was posited in Bohr's paper "On the Constitution of Atoms and Molecules," in which all atomic events are quantized, were similarly unresolvable. Both theories were true, and each disallowed the viability of the other. This is why Edward Hoffmann went to Como that September, the end of summer. To see how Bohr was going to show how two rights don't in fact make a wrong, but lead to yet another right.

Nineteen twenty-seven and we have come here to commemorate the hundredth anniversary of the death of Alessandro Volta, inventor of the electric battery, pioneer in whose honor the basic unit of electrical potential was named. Einstein, as I say, has refused to attend, does not trust Mussolini any more than he does the fledgling precepts of quantum mechanics—perhaps even less, as he surely approves of the dream of creating a coherent mathematical framework that might encompass every branch of atomic physics far above any efforts of a craven dictator whose greatest success seems to be in draining swamps.

Others of us also distrust the bright bullies who are rising into power, disregard their speeches and their tawdry credos, as we are not naive but have come because we are interested above all in pushing forward with our own, more natural, revolutions. They may try to turn us into proxy murderers in the years ahead, these bosses, but now, here in this quiet retreat by the lake, we want to listen to one another, share notes on the most private secrets nature has left to hide, and if we must put on some little show of respect for one of our mild forebears, so be it. We have nothing against Volta. He was no fascist and made his contribution to science.

What are the dualisms that make our classic and our quantum?

Great realism, the music of our ancestors Austen, Dickens, Balzac, Dostoyevsky, James, was in the time of Bohr brought into question and seen as troublingly illogical. Realism was an honest sham. Time in mimetic creation was made to look linear, which is a lie. Cause and effect were made to look nonrandom, a condition which does not exist in life. Plot, ordered and measurable as a system of manipulation, was a comely false- hood. And dialogue, in which character responds to character like tennis ball to racket over net to court to racket over net to court to racket, was a fraud. Literature should not follow but make its own wake and dust. And so it has, with triumphs and quirks and calamities.

For me, I will use anything that I find useful to see my fictive system work, will build with any apt thing around, from history to corymbs of toothpicks and painted cotton, from maps to sore feet, from quarts of crys- tals, tinnery and orchids to the whiskers of cats. Realism strikes my fancy as much as any pomo systemic, and with every novel I write I find myself won- dering more and more what value is there in any reductionism whatever.

Rancid butter may not be so good to spread on toast, but that doesn't mean it can't unstick a rusty axle. The answer, once more, is not reduction- ism but complementarity.

Nür die Fülle führt zur Klarheit *is not a retrenchment but a wider em- brace. And Bohr knew this, too, seeing complementary qualities, as another physicist has noted, "in ethics (truth as opposed to justice), in psychology (thoughts as opposed to sentiments), in biology (mechanism as opposed to vitalism)." This is why complementarity allows both art for art's sake (style over content) and a vision of politics and ethics (content over form) to exist in a given work at the same time.*

The rocks are various and jagged here along the shore, even after all these centuries of lapping water. I must be careful not to twist my ankle. Music, a waltz, floats orchestral across the lake. The stars are emerging. No moon tonight. It has been a long time since I last saw a shooting star. Is this be- cause I don't look upwards as often as I did when I was a boy?

The rhythm of lake waves lapping the scree is consistent in its irregular- ity. I am sure the random patterns of waves against beaches could be cap- tured by an equation. Seven small waves, one unexpected crashing wave and its fizzy aftermath of scuttling pebbles, then two small waves spaced well apart. Makes no sense, but the computation that would explain the phe- nomenon of waves on shores and their irregularity could be derived, no doubt. One would have to take into account total volume of water in the lake and geography of the lake's bottom. The pressure of air on the surface weighs in. It also has to do with the moon, and maybe the stars.

I make my way back to the hotel. It will be good to dream in a bed in- stead of the crowded compartment of a raucous train.

When my mother laid me down to sleep, back when I was a boy, she would tell me a bedtime story, and if the story was good, her purpose in telling me the story—which was to put me to sleep—as often as not had the opposite *result. Wide-awake, wide-eyed, I would watch her as she made up turns and twists in her plot. I listened to the music of her words. The music made me dreamy. But the story, if it moved forward, then jumped backward to pick up this strand and that, hesitated then lunged, say, if I was caught up in it, would keep me awake.*

I loved a story but knew even then in my way that the manner and method of the telling is also a story unto itself. I could never and cannot now value the one without the other, the other without the one. It would be like valuing warp over woof, or vice versa.

Waste not want not, my mother would often say. To the writer, what more sensible advice—all is useful. If it wasn't for bad luck I wouldn't have no luck at all, was written by one who knows that everything is valuable. The fiction writer's freedom to embrace linearity and at the same time the omnidirectional line of narrative, of classic and quantum, is a freedom worth seizing. Freedom to comprehend within a fictive construct a personal ethic, even as we know art answers only for itself, is a freedom to seize. Freedom to ignore the pressure any clique or ambition would impose: seize it.

Is light finally constituted of waves or of particles? The old quantum mechanist would answer that light is finally constituted of neither. Is fiction really mimetic or autoreflective? It is really neither, because it is both and yet more than both, as well. Because the fiction, when it is perceived by a reader, is passed through an entirely separate, reconstituting imagination, undergoing wholly unpredictable transformations. This is why there can never be absolute, quantitative scales with which to establish relative values of fictional work.

Nür die Fülle führt zur Klarheit: it is a phrase whose truth can never stale. "Clarity comes only from completeness." This is what I think when I wake in my horsehair bed.

Eggs poached in olive oil. Only in northern Italy can such voluptuous culinary abandon occur. Warm bread to sop the oil from this white shallow bowl. Espresso, thick juice.

The essential problem with answering such questions as where is your work leading you, where is it going, is that, of course, armed even with the best intentions and well-marked maps, one cannot know. It could be that one should not know. Rydberg's constant, I think.

We gather to listen to papers in the great ballroom that has been arranged with podium and chairs. Two blackboards, one at either side of the dais. Fermi speaks, Planck. Sunlight pours hard through the lofty windows along the southern wall of the hotel. My friends and I are in the last row of seats. We sit up straight and listen to the morning lectures.

After lunch, Bohr stands before the congress and uses words such as *renunciation* and phrases such as *certain general point of view* that would reconcile mutually exclusive results as equally valid. An unscientific smile lifts at the corners of my mouth even as I struggle to follow him through a lightening labyrinth of proofs.

The newly discovered cave paintings of horses and bison and owls and hyenas at Chauvet are reassuring—thirty thousand years old and with lines that would make Gaudier blush and Sesshu bow—in that they (mutely) speak once more of the fallacy of progressive development in the arts. Science may well be less fundamental than art, since it does progress.

Eschatologists concern themselves with the study of last things, historians with what has come before. Novelists are mythmakers interested in both. They conceive a middle, the fantastic now, a continuance fabricated with language and proposing narratives that may or may not have taken place, historically speaking, but which become part of social history in the same way memoir does, or biography, or history itself, or really any expression that is preserved—like a painting in a cave, say.

Shamans have always been middlemen. Magicians dignified by the social purpose of their mischief, a function that extends beyond diversion and messes with souls and spirits. Novelists and mythmakers, even those who try their best to erase narrative and who reject the word as univocal signifier, are shamanistic insofar as they, too, are infatuated by the middle.

Writings on a cave wall, hidden from history down in the darkness of the middle world.

Complementarity introduced an axiom of ambiguity into the system of physical science, and this did not sit well with many of the older physicists who were in the room that day. Renunciation—a quite unscientific term for the necessary gesture—was not what scientists practiced, as a rule, and the mood at dinner that night was such that I could not stay in the room. Bohr sat at a table with Heisenberg nearby, arguing with Schrödinger, Planck, and Rutherford, as friends might, long after the dishes had been cleared and the cigars and brandy served, but I had to get back out to the shore, to walk and clear my head.

The stones under my feet clacked and rattled hollowly just as they had the night before. I looked out over the water and could hear, again this evening, more music, a song by Debussy. A woman sang, accompanied by piano, and I could hear the words,

Le sceptre des rivages roses
Stagnants sur les soirs d'or, ce l'est,
Ce blanc vol fermé que tu poses
Contre le feu. . . .

No lovers rowed on the lake, though I could discern wave patterns on the water that resembled very much the wake that little boat had made before. I took them for a *complementum.*

The physicist and fabulist are both magicians, but rather than dealing in sleight of hand, they are bent upon pulling real doves out of real hats, doves that weren't in those hats before.
     Doves truly plucked out of empty air.
     Those things which seem most utterly in apposition are where, as Bohr has said, the work begins. And so I have come to understand that what interests me more than to debunk or ignore traditional forms, is to transubstantiate them. This is nothing new, but nothing is. History is always a form of invention.

Work took me from England to Geneva. When the war began, I moved to New York and eventually resided in Baltimore, where I was born—a stubborn, resolving circle of a life. I heard Bohr lecture in Brussels in the early thirties. He hadn't aged a day. Still the same slow, methodical, thoughtful, pained sentences he used to mediate impossible abstract paths. Bohr's call for synthesis had borne many fruits, and quantum theory was by then an important branch of physics. A viable model for the atom was complete and already ways of deriving energy from its manipulation were being studied by Leo Szilard and others. Los Alamos, high in the Jemez Mountains of northern New Mexico, was no longer a boy's ranch. Bohr would go there under the code name Baker.
     I married, became a chemical engineer, and registered several patents. I lived my life. After I became ill and was diagnosed with cancer, a mutual friend of mine and Michele Besso wrote me, and quoted from a letter Einstein had forwarded to his widow after hearing of his old friend's death. Einstein, who himself had but a few weeks to live, had by then finally admitted that there might be something to quantum theory and complementarity, though he'd never pursued any serious work about either. Still, he spoke of the meaninglessness of death with such apprehending strength. It doesn't mean a thing, death, he wrote. For those of us who believe in physics, this separation between past, present, and future is only an illusion, however tenacious.
     This was just the sort of composite picture of meaning in life and work, art and death, I had always tried in my way to embrace.

31 Questions and Statements about the Future of Literary Publishing, Bookstores, Writers, Readers, and Other Matters

John O'Brien

1. THIS IS NOW ALMOST old hat, at least in some circles. The future bookstore will consist of as many as 200,000 sample books (all strategically chained to a rack so that no one walks off with them), not representing every book ever published (maybe not even representing every book currently "in print") but still a very healthy sampling of almost anything you might want to browse through. At the center of this store will be something resembling a Kinko's. If you want a hard copy of the book you browsed through, an hour later you will pick it up; at the very worst, it will look like what bound book galleys currently look like (paperbound on plain white paper, with little more than the title of the book and author on the cover). Or you may still yearn for the nineteenth century and want your book bound in leather (well, imitation leather) because your library at home is all in burgundy leather (imitation, that is), and you want your personal library to color-co-ordinate with your couch (books have many uses). The book you have just purchased would have been unavailable to you ten years before; it was out of print, and even your public library did not have a copy. Now you find it under "French Fiction" in your convenient Blockbuster-like bookstore. As you walk out of this store, you wonder why it is not possible for you to download at home, print on your high-speed, 600 dpi printer, and bind the book with your personalized covers that you keep in a box next to your computer. Well, wait another few years, and you will be able to do this. The Library of Congress will be in your living room.

2. Or you want to read on-screen. Welcome to it. What is the screen? A small, book-shaped screen (double-sided), with contrast and definition that, well, resembles a book (I have Evelin Sullivan to thank for this). Or maybe you want to read from a big screen. Your choice. The consumer is in control at last. Or say you got the disk from the store in #1. As the middlemen drop by the wayside, the cost of all of this also drops. Why must we now pay $25 for a book? Not because of the cost of producing the book; we pay $25 so that everyone along the way can get his cut, as inadequate as that cut may be. No one wants to consider what the actual costs are; no one, especially

the publisher, wants to consider this because it raises the question of what need there is, or isn't, for all the middlemen, including—as presently constituted—the publisher.

3. What will cause #1 & 2 to happen? As always in America, especially in America, they will be caused by money. The $25 book will no longer cost the consumer $25, and yet someone will still find a way of becoming a billionaire by reducing the cost to the consumer (e.g., the guy who makes those imitation-leather covers). What else creates this change? The other half of saving money: the technology is there, though the book industry is the slowest "business" in America to respond to new technology. (After all these years, why are books still not sold or widely promoted on television? We now have specialty cable stations for almost everything, except . . . let's not get into it.)

4. Cultural effects? Enormous. All books, all information, all whatever will be available to everyone at all times. You live in some awful town in Arkansas? Well, you still have all books available in your living room, bookstore, or library (imagine a library very much like the bookstore I described). Even in Arkansas. Suffer from isolation? Not if you are hooked up to reading groups on the Internet, one of which may even exist for Gilbert Sorrentino. Gilbert Sorrentino himself might be part of the group. Or maybe not. In any event, you are now hooked up to everything and everyone. Even in Arkansas.

5. Most people will say that this can't happen. Why? Because they want to read books only in the form that they've always enjoyed. But won't having the books bound (if this is what they want) be enough? No, they say, they want to get them in the ways they have always gotten them. We can put these people in the category of those who said in the late forties and early fifties (I remember well) that they would never get a television because nothing could replace the radio. Even within my Irish-Catholic ghettoized neighborhood of Chicago (a two-square-mile neighborhood that some residents had not stepped out of all of their lives: born there, baptized there, confirmed there, married there, and would be buried there—if they were males, they had stepped out for military service and, perhaps, their daily jobs), all households had televisions by the midfifties. Radio got changed, as we know. Most people said the same thing about color television. Then VCRs. Then cable. Books have been the most resistant to change (was the first book written, then published, then read by Republicans?). In any event, such responses are not worth listening to. Ten dollars for a book at the Kinko/Blockbuster bookstore or $50 at the local old-fashioned store that is about to go out of business? End of argument—especially in America.

6. Will our age be the end of reading and the end of "stories"? No. We will change the forms, but the need for stories remains. But will the need for reading remain? Yes, until some other human activity can fulfill the same need for quiet meditation with language and the imagination that is the act of reading. But what new form? The old form, the first form of the Word, was the oral storyteller. Mass reading occurred only when (again, of course, because of technology) books could be mass produced, and when that fact coincided with the rise of the middle class (again, of course, money) and the possibility of leisure, and therefore education, etc. I don't know what reading's future form will be. Quite likely not a return to bards wandering from town to town (though in fact we might be seeing a return to the oral tradition via books-on-tape), and perhaps the transformation could be as slight as from book to portable computer that *looks* like a book. Humans can, despite our experience of them, be quite adaptable.

7. What of experimental fiction? It will go on, as it always has, beneath the surface, behind the scenes, completely removed from the interests of the masses as well as the interests of most intellectuals and academics. The demand for it will neither greatly expand nor much decrease. Like the poor, it is always with us. Some experimental fiction will be good and will last, and will finally, as always, be integrated into the mainstream; some will be bad and will die, as it always has. Will most people—especially those at the hippest cutting edge of the culture—continue to hate it and dismiss it? Yes, of course. The body culture will always attack it as a foreign invader.

8. What will the fiction of the future be like? This is not the domain of critics. Writers will decide this, just as they always have.

9. Will John Updike be remembered a hundred years from now? John who? Even so, his books will be electronically available.

10. What is the relationship between commercial publishers and nonprofit literary presses? The question really is: What will commercial publishing be doing with literary books in, let's say, fifteen years? Let's look at what it has done with poetry, as well as drama, in the last twenty-five years and then project this onto fiction. Today, except in unusual cases, highly literary fiction does not sell well enough to justify the expenses of commercial publishing; just how badly it sells is a trade secret, but the range (except for unusual circumstances, the Pulitzer, for example) is between 2,000 and 7,500 copies of a given book. The old, now dying system was that a commercial publisher would "invest" in a young writer because one day he/she would write a breakthrough novel that would catapult him/her onto the best-seller list, win awards, and become a prestigious part of the publisher's corporate image. The old system continues, or staggers on, to the present

day, but with steadily fewer risks taken, less investment, less interest in *that* kind of corporate image.

Let's compare all of this to changes in the business of baseball. Even after clubs were moving into the new age of agents, multimillion dollar player contracts, nine-figure broadcast deals with networks, etc. (keeping in mind that it wasn't too many years ago that no games except the All-Star Game and the World Series were nationally televised, and that, even on a local level, the decision to televise home games was the choice of the owners and whether they thought this would interfere with gate-paying customers), and clubs began to operate as true businesses rather than being the expensive hobbies of chewing gum magnates, you can be sure that a tradition such as "Ladies Day" (whereby women, in order to woo them to an interest in baseball, or at least to get them to tolerate their husbands' interest, were offered free admission) continued. Only after some years did someone realize that most women were now coming to games because of the entertainment, the hipness of—let's say—Cubbies baseball, the fireworks, the clowns, the hoopla; in short, because of the game's status as social-entertainment event. No need to let them in free, especially since corporations were now buying the box seats and the skyboxes and whatever else; no reason to have to worry about the women (i.e., housewives) who had nothing better to do on a Friday afternoon and who, if they couldn't come along, might interfere with their husbands' and kids' attendance.

This is essentially the same relation that literary fiction has to commercial publishing. Why do it? The tradition staggers on (as did Ladies Day) in order to satisfy editors who are bringing in money from other books, staggers on to satisfy the needs of conscience, and staggers on so that there can be awards and prizes and puffery. (How do you have awards for O. J. books, the Pope's book, or Tom Clancy? You can't, unless you consent to become entirely like the rest of the entertainment industry, namely, television and Hollywood and pop music.) The end of literary books in commercial publishing is a historical inevitability, slow to occur only because publishing has always been a nineteenth-century contraption that, even today, depends upon having sales reps going door-to-door to stores where they build relationships and try to be well-liked.

Twenty-five years ago, every respectable New York (or Boston) publishing house published poetry and translations, and most of them published plays. Is there any commercial house that does plays any longer? Fewer and fewer do translations, and fewer and fewer do poetry, and those that continue to do poetry books do fewer of them and now tend to favor poets who collect Social Security checks and who, God knows, won't sell very well but will get respectable reviews (that is, in the three or four reviews that the *New York Times* does each year in its roundup of poetry books). Poetry has almost entirely fallen to university and nonprofit presses; plays don't get published, unless by Theatre Communications Group (a nonprofit publisher); and literary fiction is, well . . . continuing, sort of. Serious books and interesting new authors are published in New York—Gaddis, Millhauser, David Foster Wallace, William T. Vollmann, Richard Powers, William Burroughs, John Barth, Joyce Carol Oates, Saul Bellow, John Updike (God help us—you can see, I am casting the net wide and am willing to count Updike among "serious writers," if not very good ones), and so on. It's Ladies Day, folks. Do not think that QVC-Paramount-AT&T-Fox-Murdoch, Inc. will have this go on much longer. Why would they? And if you think they will, then you believe that they are just about to start supporting ballet and opera, which is the cultural and financial equivalent to some of the writers I've named above.

And so? Literary fiction will eventually become the domain of nonprofit publishers and university publishers (though the latter is a strange category: some still do not even put the price of the book on the jacket!). And so? And so either these publishers will be able to take on this cultural responsibility or they won't. And they will be able to take it on only if they have the dollars (these are not the best of economic days for university presses to be expanding lists, especially in the area of literary fiction).

11. It's best not to get married. This has nothing to do with the above but is worthwhile advice to the youth.

12. Why didn't North Point Press survive? Because it was, almost from the start and despite attempts to change in the end, trying both to be a literary publisher *and* to make money. The two are not compatible, as everyone knows. (In fact, publishing itself does not make money, but not everyone knows this. How many fortunes have been lost in commercial New York publishing? Let's not get into this one. Ask Jim Sitter. Publishing will one day make money but only as part of a much larger entertainment network. Believe it.) At any rate, North Point could not sell enough copies of people like Gilbert Sorrentino and Juan Goytisolo. It should have been a nonprofit press. Since foundations were not, and largely still are not funding literary publishing, this probably would not have made a difference, but at least North Point would have known what they were up against. What of North Point's two best-sellers? Such things create more problems than they solve (that is, they don't solve any problems). In brief, best-sellers cost a lot of money, and you had better have the staff to handle them, and then you had better not make the mistake of thinking that you can keep duplicating the process.

13. Does it make any difference whether literature survives? Maybe not, but only in the sense that to people alive right now, it may not make any difference whether the environment survives; they won't be around to choke on the water or to breathe in pure CO. Both literature and the environment have to do with the quality of life, as do music, ballet, museums. We can, of course, survive without ballet, but survive to do what?

14. Is literature relevant to anything? A number of novels by African-Americans (dear God, this term is back in use: will politics in America ever make up its mind?), culminating in *Native Son* and *Invisible Man,* caused the civil rights movement in this country. No one will agree with this and I don't want to spend the time arguing it. Or: Hemingway's fiction *created* the American male. Again, I don't have the time. Emerson created a number of things, most of them either bad or badly misapplied (that toad of a man Newt Gingrich would not be possible without Emerson, nor would Dr. Strangelove [aka Bob Dole] have been possible).

15. How could America produce such a pure product as Jesse Helms? Or Dan Quayle?

16. Why are children the least protected group in America? They have no money and no votes. Why are the elderly next? They don't have enough money and may not be able to vote. And the poor? Enough said. And we ask why literary fiction will cease to be published by commercial houses?

17. Why are small presses almost always begun by people who are difficult to get along with? Why do they always impress other people as cranks?

18. If nonprofit literary publishers are to assume the responsibility of making literature a viable cultural force in America, they need money. They need money to become stable and institutionalized; they need money for marketing so that the books will reach readers; they need money to pay writers; and they need money to pay the printing bills. Philanthropists, are you listening?

19. Who is Tim Robbins? Who is Jim Sitter?

20. Will more fiction be reviewed in the *New York Times* now that Chip McGrath is the editor? Yes.

21. Is it true that the *Atlantic Monthly* has become a totally irrelevant magazine? The answer to this is yes.

22. When the idea for *Vanity Fair* was first floated almost a year before the first issue appeared, was it to have a heavy emphasis upon things literary? Yes. But by the date of publication, the accountants had figured out that this was not the way to go.

23. Do you remember the days when the *Chicago Sun-Times* had a real Sunday book section? You must be well above forty if you remember such days. Is this part of a conspiracy to keep Chicago forever the Second City?

24. Are young editors required to know the work of Edward Dahlberg, Douglas Woolf, Jack Spicer, Carl Van Vechten, Dorothy Richardson, John Dos Passos, and Chandler Brossard? You must be kidding. Must they even know the names so as to be able to answer whether these people are plumbers or writers? You must be kidding. Can one be a good editor without knowing the complete work of Edward Dahlberg? No. Can one be an influential editor without ever having heard of Edward Dahlberg? Emphatically yes.

25. With what kind of reason do publishers hate writers? A good one. Do publishers want to be thought of as people who hate writers? Never.

26. Do people want to think of publishing as a noble profession? A gentleman's profession? Yes, they do. Are a lot of people deluded about many things? Yes, they are.

27. Should our federal government, as do many other governments, pay for the publication of the country's literary heritage? Yes, it should. Especially when Newt Gingrich is a novelist in his own right. Should America be embarrassed because it does not pay for such a thing? Yes.

28. America needs a review source for books that is completely independent of commercial interests. Such a publication (or perhaps it should be on television or radio) must gather the best critical minds in the country. It must *not* be supported by advertising from publishers. It must be widely distributed, perhaps given away rather than sold. Such a review source could change the face of publishing in America. Philanthropists, are you listening?

29. Would the word *smug* adequately describe the demeanor and attitude of John Updike? Yes.

30. The purest form of American censorship is reducing books to their marketplace value. Most affected are literary books, but of course any books that, at the moment, have limited sales potential are so censored. It is the most effective form of censorship ever known because it makes so much common (i.e., economic) sense to Americans. If Newt Gingrich thought that the fiction of Edward Dahlberg was unavailable because it was being *censored,* then he would be at the front of massive protests in Washington (well, I know this isn't true, but you see what I mean). Literature thrived in Eastern Europe during state-imposed censorship, but stopped thriving as soon as the marketplace began to take over. Should it matter to anyone how many books are not available to them? If they weren't available because of state censorship, it would matter. But what is the difference? The countervoices are silenced all the same. College students have available to them

only what commercial publishers make available and what will sell well enough to justify being kept in print. The Republic is not in good shape nor is it protected when language is equated with commodity. Someone's interests are protected (and of course someone is making money), but the interests of the Republic are not protected. Literature would thrive in America if only the government would begin to have book burnings and imprison writers! A new Golden Age! Gilbert Sorrentino would be the most read writer in America. Instead, the Republic yawns. "If the damn book were any good, then people would buy it!"

31. I had intended that there be only 27 questions and statements. But, along the way, I had wanted to make a comment about marriage, and once I had made one comment about John Updike, I could not resist another. There may also be other extraneous remarks here.

Specially Marked Packages

Christopher Sorrentino

THE INTENSITY WITH which those who ache to brand literature obsolete have seized upon newer electronic media as its usurpers is deeply suspect, mostly because the story's old news that was wrong when it was fresh. The impulse to mourn one form's death in the aftermath of another's advent seems to stem from somewhat silly and reductive cause-and-effect reasoning that posits "progress" in any given area as a development occurring in a vacuum and spreading its effects definitively, but only over a limited area. Only occasionally is the possibility that "conventional" fiction writers might apply the techniques and the very technology of such emergent media toward a recrudescence of the much maligned avant-garde ever addressed. It's a rather disheartening indication of the way in which the garbled Darwinian principles of The Marketplace have taken root and spread throughout all aspects of the culture: naturally, the loudest discussion of the fabled decline of interest in the printed word generally is carried on by such obviously transient media exempla as mainstream magazines and newspapers—which also perpetuate the most hilariously earnest investigations of The New (i.e., newly popular), from CD-ROMs to hypertext to the Internet to the scarily (to them) haphazard (ditto) demographics of the zines. The fact is that there is no limit to the varieties of art that can coexist. Its most "evolved" forms sit side by side with its most "primitive": nothing so backwards as painting a picture, but the blank surface is attacked by fresh minds every day.

But then, the idea always has been to lay the blame for literature's lack of popularity on electronic straw men, especially television. To argue otherwise would be to imply that the majority of people are too lazy and undisciplined to read literature; and that television's development (i.e., "Television") walks in lockstep with the moribund progress of their gross intellectual lassitude, both of which assertions are surely true.[1] Far easier

---

[1]Although it's only fair to say that I think it requires the utmost in myopic partisan conceit to make the claim that literature's products are inherently more sublimely creative than those of television—and I don't mean the medium itself, all that stupid palaver about "untapped potential" (which totally misses the point that television's potential of delivering demographically suitable audiences to advertisers was realized long ago and is continually being refined), I mean plain old TV: the dumbest shows on television, and certainly any commercial, are better, use techniques and

to sneak such scabrousness in through the back door: while it is certainly the case that literature is held in contempt, the official perception is really exactly the opposite: adrift in a state of economic languor—as opposed to TV's robust ability to cause money and goods to change hands—literature is subject to a kind of phony exaltation, which effectively elevates it to a station of complete impotence. In this sense, literature's position of every-day influence over the culture is that of the model figurehead: quiet, polite, available to be hauled out for every occasion, and now and then a source of profit. The People throw up their hands: good-natured admissions all around that literature is better than they are, just as they always suspected; now they can ignore it in the state of grace conferred by having had the best intentions.

If the bestowal upon literature of Sick Man of Art status (so what else is new?) indicates anything, though, it is probably that the publishing industry will have to examine new ways of packaging and selling books. What is it about fiction that places it at such a remove from the consumer, anyway? The merchandise is stackable, portable, durable, relatively inexpensive, and lends itself to attractive packaging. Who the hell knows? It's difficult. It tends to remain completely inert when one is not devoting 100 percent to reading it. The reward derived from that 100 percent effort is portrayed as negligible—i.e., it is inconvertibly itself, and cannot be transmuted into anything more useful.

There's also the possibility that in a society as deracinated and stripped of tradition and continuity—by jet travel, the automobile, the interstate highway system, corporate relocations, urban sprawl (i.e., white flight), chain stores, divorce, staggering incarceration rates, etc.—as our own, the void that emptily exists where common experience would ordinarily repose is filled by elements of popular culture so anchored to a specific time that they become part of the lingua franca, staples of the manufactured conver-sation, endlessly in medias res, that takes the place of shared heritage. In effect, trends in television, movies, and popular music and fake nostalgia for their various incarnations are our shared conscious heritage (in other words, Nick at Nite is not kidding), in a way that literature can never be, since fiction blasts aside most temporal restrictions with its persistent *avail-ability,* as opposed to the *unavoidability* of popular culture, the availability of whose specific manifestations is strictly controlled—thus its association with a time, a place, a hairstyle, a mode of fashion.[2]

---

methods that are by their very nature decades fresher, than the average book that gets a favorable review in the *Times.*

[2]N.B.: whether this latter fact will change in the face of the new Digital/Interactive/ Multimedia era is open to debate—and certainly the idea of "choice" is the market-ing buzzword of the day—to which possibility I can say only that such visions have always been demonstrably utopian. A show of hands: Who remembers when cable

It could also be that while at one time mental digestion (or rejection) of whatever esoteric pleasures the book contained between its covers may have been the objective (for whatever reasons), this is an increasingly irrelevant and rarefied end, consigned to the specialists (frequently scumbags), since the idea of "knowledge" and its synthesis has been largely replaced by "information"—inviolable manna from above, relevant and necessary. We constantly read and hear middlebrow complaints about the burdens attendant upon life in the Information Age—"All that darn information!"—the unaddressed corollary to this pathetic hand-wringing bitch being that the vast bulk of the proffered info is sheerest bullshit and broken glass. "Commercial Media" makes its provisions for a deceptively exclusive discourse in which only the dominant and hegemonic elements of the society are given full voice. This voice is used to impart information concerning what to buy, where to go, what to eat, etc. The exceptional is buried beneath the gleaming representation of the fashionable, the relative novelty of which lends it the cloak of exceptionality. Scumbags, generally affiliated with either sundry academies or the mainstream press, set up cottage industries to reassure us about how exceptional the fashionable is. Since fashion demands, by its very nature, that news of its Kallikak-like mutations be disseminated with a certain alacrity, other media are given priority over print.

So there is this immediate distance between the consumer and that unknown silent timeless object, aka "book." For the most part one doesn't read *Light in August* and then discuss it at the watercooler the next day. To this extent, at least, fiction is incapable of serving the "social" purpose we demand, in the absence of our souls, from our divertissements.

The problems seem to be pretty clear, when distilled. Difficult, useless utterances in an alien and/or alienated tongue, quite simply unconcerned with the simple exchange of goods, delivered inefficiently and without any uniformity as to time and place of dissemination to serve as communal aspic—in the piquant phrase used by one of my old lawyer cronies to describe court trials in which exhibits were nothing more invigorating than blow-ups of balance sheets, not "sexy." Writers know all of this, of course; they are rather un-"sexy" people. They spend lambent, warm afternoons sequestered in quiet rooms. They devote days to tuning a sentence which, in finished form, will sell nothing to no one. They urge the most wrenching revelations out of themselves and then throw them in the wastepaper basket, or cover them with cryptic scrawled corrective sigla like a suit marked for alteration. The spontaneity and fun that major advertisers urge upon us have nothing to do with the Sisyphean labors of the writer, who rolls a stone to the top of the hill to discover a Coke-swilling, Nike-shod adventurer parked at its summit in a Jeep.

---

television was going to democratize the medium, ushering in a golden age of daring, literate, commercial-free programming?

That's why writers contractually cede all responsibility in this respect to the Big Boys, the Experts, the Professionals manning the awesome marketing and promotional guns at Advance, Paramount, Time-Warner, et al. If anyone's in a position to crack the mystery—sheer overhead aside—of why a movie that five million people go to see is a bomb yet a novel that sells a hundred thousand hardcover copies is a best-seller, it's them. We're all counting on them to figure this stuff out for us. It's obvious that *popular* fiction somehow manages to overcome the hurdles faced by literary fiction. It definitely has its "moment," it definitely becomes the subject of those watercooler chats. But most such books sell themselves to an audience that berates itself for indulging in guilty pleasures—no surprise in a society that has come to equate nonconsumptive (act of purchase in this case notwithstanding) leisure time with frivolity. Currently, though, a peculiar alchemy appears to be taking place: the literary novel is gradually being transformed into the popular novel, while the popular novel is now, more often than not, backed by the full faith and credit of the mainstream critical establishment—i.e., whether the verdict is positive or not, the thing is dealt with as a work deserving serious consideration. The golden mean, of course, is an attractive, "relevant," undemanding package designed to fly off the shelves. It's akin to decking out any shitty car in spoilers, mag wheels, sport stripes, tinted windows, a contoured "cockpit" with a lotta gauges, etc. It's an idea that's almost sublime in its blatant contempt for the people it's devised to trap, admirably corrupt and bitterly effective. Once upon a time the parvenu, the photographer's subject, the official spokesman of the newsreel and the public service film, stood and talked and gestured before meticulously shelved job lots of handsome leather bindings, bought by the pound, blank and insignificant except as an imposing symbol of his own illumination. (If you don't believe me about the durable appeal of this type of horseshit, check out the ad, probably in this Sunday's *Parade* magazine, for the Franklin Mint-style commemorative leather-bound "classics," or take a syndicated gander at John Forsythe devising ruthless corporate strategy within the sanctum of the Carrington library.) But for the most part, the patent anonymity of such objects was and is anathema to both manufacturer and consumer. I'm looking at the dust jackets of two new(er) books that are stacked on my coffee table—I mean, they really are stacked; I don't actually have to look at either jacket entire because the elements of design at work here are analogous to the endless repetitions of fractal geometry, they're all fluorescent color and pseudo-sloppy typography. The texts themselves: unimportant. All commercially published books are "coffee-table books" now. The package is the thing, and its message should be delivered efficiently and unequivocally, more potent than a stupid little beard or a pair of Doc Martens or a Land Rover in the urban First World. They're the sorts of books to be seen on the subway and in the coffeehouse with, banderole across the jacket highlighting the stupefied daily hack's usual vain grope for eloquence ("A *Catcher in the Rye* for the 80s, the 90s, the millennium. . . .").

"Generation X, right?" Well, yes—right now. Gen X is surely passing strange—I mean, at the very least its members will all be dead one day—but the means by which it has been brought to us in living color, become the subject of "heated" "debate" (cf. my comment re commercial media's deceptively exclusive discourse), and through it all sold, sold, sold (the *SF Weekly* reported in its 10 August 1994 edition that an unidentified national wholesaler cited figures indicating that so-called Generation X authors sell "between four and ten times as many books as young novelists who avoid Gen X packaging") presages a solid gold future. The component elements of a prototypical fictional chassis have been assembled out of the usual rotting garbage, spruced up with a fresh coat of paint. Many of the books currently being manufactured as part of a "Generation X" "movement" have at their dead cold centers the vacillating heart of the advertising executive. Kept aloft—that is, "relevant"—by a constant barrage of moronic platitudes concerning the meaninglessness of life (as if this were a new discovery), the emptiness of the sexual relationship (the latter-day democratization of whose romantic aspects is a dwindling luxury afforded by high capitalism's temporary redistribution of wealth), the absence of God (though most of the writers would seem to prefer Dickinson's *ignis fatuus* to the rigors of religion and faith or even a coherent moral philosophy), the impersonality of city life (the writers are by and large the pure products of Middle America—i.e., out of their element), they are really the stylized articulation of the anxious "concerns" of the postsuburban American middle class (in what might be defined as the Ur Generation X novel, 1984's *Bright Lights, Big City,* the narrator immediately reveals that what the second-person protagonist—implicitly the reader—really desires is reentry into the world of middlebrow pleasures: a Ralph Lauren Sunday brunch of croissants, the *Times,* and a nice clean girl), more akin to the brittle cardiganed output of Updike and Cheever (who are at least honest in their work about being square) than to the "hip" oeuvre with which the work insists upon affinity and from which it borrows surface movement and flash. Clotted with brand names (for the lofty sake of verisimilitude and immediacy, of course), such stuff is a perfect medium for the sort of product placement that rightly ought to command a fee, and one day routinely will. "Commercial Media's" enthusiastic embrace of what is frequently referred to as "irony" (but is really simple sarcasm) is what you could call enlightened self-deprecation. The positioning of Brand X or Brand Y on the kitchen table of one of the meaningless loveless Godless alienated characters appears as a transcendent metonym for that meaninglessness, etc., but ultimately serves as an augury of the way out. The casual, nearly perfunctory, sometimes sneering reference is really an homage: in vibrant repose beneath the hard kernel of the text is a sense not of disenfranchisement but of thwarted satisfaction.

Ah, yes—there's the rub. It's not simply a new kind of blemish on the soul of letters that's manifesting itself, but the early stages of a metastatic disease which will no doubt alter "fiction" and "literature"—at least the kind you can walk into a bookstore and buy—for good. The idea of the familiar, chunky, clunky medium itself vanishing beyond a horizon of oscillating pixels and squawking interactivity is merely a red herring. Now that its feet are wet, fiction shows all the signs of plopping its ass down in the same exploitative, collaborationist muck TV, movies, and slick magazines have long lolled in.

This is a perfectly understandable development given that fiction's relationship to the consumer has always been, at best, allusive. Generation X fiction's mimetic presentation of certain familiar aspects of middle-class life—and no matter how outré or bohemian, that is what they are—has so far sufficed only to "bring characters to life"; i.e., to humanize and affirm patterns of behavior which are the inhuman by-products of the centrifugal force exerted by capitalism's great and perpetual machine. The problem being that fiction's great evocative strengths are no match for the follow-the-dots logic of electronic visual media. Merely citing the name and properties of a given product within the context of a form that permits its creator to don endless disguises and requires its partaker to imagine every aspect of what each word signifies is not enough to do much more than sustain the momentum that product has gathered.

Thus, while the establishment of demographics-driven fiction, a generational *cosa nostra* fully equipped with its own shibboleths (some of which are thoughtfully provided in the margins), is a good first step, it merely maintains the status quo. The inroads that must be made in order for fiction to continue to justify its bottom line are yet to come. But come they will: the author will become that peculiar creature, the celebrity. The perfect antidote to mass production and the genuine sense of alarm it is likely to engender is the maintenance of the illusion of uniqueness via the creation of surplus celebrity. One of the key objectives of popular culture is to transform the unknown into the celebrity, and the celebrity into the authority. Somewhere in this equation, the ideal of artistry is lost, since the perfect celebrity is really an entertainer: the artist's logical replacement in our time. This entertainer is never offstage, is obliged to suffer the imposition of strangers' expectations upon his life. There is something that he "does," some basis for the fact of his stature (he acts, plays professional sports, sings, eats shit and barks at the moon), and we play at evaluating this stuff objectively, ranking him against predecessors and peers, comparing poor performances with superior ones. It is known to all at some gut level that the performance is merely the tail that wags the dog, that this person's persistent occupation of our consciousness is the result of something else altogether. One admires, say, Michael Jordan for parlaying his rather marginalized ability into a multimillion-dollar annual income, and admires him for the ability itself. But ultimately, "Michael Jordan" is chimerical, and what one admires is the management of various corporate entities. Despite himself, Michael Jordan becomes the embodiment of capitalist transubstantiation as it creates newer and better spectacles with which to sell more product. Fifty years ago few people cared about, and fewer "needed," professional basketball. But basketball is evidently an able prophet of breakfast flakes and sneakers, and its larger-than-life incarnation is the human being named Michael Jordan.

Interestingly, Jordan's temporary retirement from the game spared him (and cost him) nothing. Even as society itself has fragmented into increasingly meaningless enclaves of specialization, the business of the celebrity has become one of resolute diversification. What the avatar exemplifies becomes the seal and crest entitling him to go on to write, act, tutor others in health and fitness, enter politics—or serve as the "credible spokesperson." (Not that this is altogether unexpected in a society whose greatest celebrity, Jesus Christ, tacitly endorses any and all products between the day after Thanksgiving and December 25. Like all cynical campaigns, Operation Jesus is loaded with public service messages—Peace on Earth, etc.—in the fine print at the bottom of the pitch. Jesus rarely appears in the ads, but it's understood that merchants speak ex cathedra.)

The author, then. The author of the future will of needs be as famous as any star we wish upon today. The author of the future will endorse products as a matter of course, appear on slick magazine covers, perform on broadcast and cable "spoken word" telecasts, provide fodder for gossip columnists, hope for an acting career, and host *Saturday Night Live*. Meanwhile, the creator's license to vanish from sight within the work will be suspended. In fact, the creator and the work must become synonymous. What the creator/work *says,* in what will doubtless be its nutty, irreverent, rebellious way, will call into question every institution and tradition and decorous trope of the legendary "mainstream," which waits like a sitting duck on some imaginary Front Porch of America in tacky polyester so garish that it screams its way right through the sepia tone.[3] But it will simply be

---

[3]An aside: naturally, such work will continue the current trend of "past-ing" imagery, which will progress so that anything existing prior to the present will lose all credibility. Any image can be presented straight-faced as a fragment of another time while the overlaid narrative prompts our perception of it as the embodiment of that time's foolish inferiority to our own (commercial representations of an idealized present day, of course, are given us as accurate in their depiction of our lives). The mercantile implications of condemning as simpler, blander, and more homogeneous whatever can thus be characterized are clear: our own present becomes a parallel and vastly superior universe existing contemporaneously with that of the moving, audible past. In fact, given that such images from, say, the fifties are culled from a popular culture which felt little pressure to represent a "diverse" society or to address "issues" or to approach its goals of maximum individual consumption in any but the most straightforward terms, we are nearly obligated to assume a certain moral high-handedness when reflecting upon the follies of the past.

another depressingly familiar David Letterman routine, in which the wealthy and famous nudge each other in the ribs and then go out for a drink together. To make art is to be innovative, to be innovative is first to question the way things are, and then to change them. The tremendous, bitter irony of Irony, Inc. is that its satire is so benign, and the forms that contain it so conventional, that Douglas Coupland has been put on MTV's payroll, and Henry Rollins and Tama Janowitz both are getting dough from Apple Computer. Granted, these are "cool" products—which is merely more evidence of the sleight of hand that dazzles us day after day after day. If Henry Rollins hawked exercise machines or protein powder on TV in the dead of night he might conceivably earn the opprobrium and ridicule of all the people who think the PowerBook ads are "cool." But he knows this, and so does Apple, so Henry can appear aloofly individualist, computer tucked under his tattooed oxter, all the while receiving a good fuck up the ass from the powers that be. Naturally, the writers who sacrifice voice for persona— i.e., become entertainers—will enjoy shortened careers, having placed themselves in thrall to the public and its fickle desires. Their work, informed by the need to please many, will cease to have any integrity whatsoever. Since its message will be only that of what it sells, it will be instantly replaceable.

From a marketing and sales standpoint, this will represent a vast improvement over the methods of the past. Getting the writers to fit snugly into the corporate pocket will require a little outlay, but it's worth it. A book always could hit big in the cross-cultural sense that matters nowadays, but it was a hit-or-miss affair. Take it from an expert: "After 1957 *On the Road* sold a trillion levis [*sic*] and a million espresso coffee machines, and also sent countless kids on the road. This was of course due in part to the media, the arch-opportunists. They know a story when they see one." That's William Burroughs, "cult" figure and corporate spokesman, measuring the ultimate impact of Kerouac's famous novel. The remark was delivered long before Burroughs himself became an "arch-opportunist" and sold out to Nike, Inc., and its trenchant edge is somewhat blunted by the passage of time, but rehoned by first peering through a lens in which the world appears as a place where blue jeans are work clothes and coffee tasteless muck ruined in a percolator and then turning away to confront the ubiquity of jeans and the familiar names, like McDonald's, selling espresso on every 1990s street. Momentarily inhabiting the mind of the huckster, one sees the possibilities of the world refreshed, sees doors swinging wide open. One of the great truisms of our time is that anything can be used to sell anything. Kerouac's vision was swiftly distilled into iconographic staples by those arch-opportunists; to this day blue jeans, for example, are pitched as the garb of "the rebel"—despite the fact that they are possibly the only item of apparel in history to transcend age, race, gender, class, financial status, and the various "poses" of its wearers in its appeal—in advertisements replete with

Open Road imagery and occasionally quite noisy intimations of sex and intoxication.

Meanwhile, the work is absolutely secondary: *On the Road* remains in print but, for good or ill, it has been overtaken and possessed by its own distorted likeness. The archetypal "beat" existent in the collective consciousness bears more of a resemblance to Bob Denver than to Neal Cassady, and the "lifestyle" he celebrates is a fully accessorized caricature more at home on Madison Avenue than on Route 66. The most recent edition of the book (Penguin) that I've seen finalizes the insult: on its cover is the famous photograph of Cassady and Kerouac, standing side by side. Kerouac is reduced to a co-starring role in his own book, the book is reduced to Kerouac's statement, and the statement is reduced to "Jeans Are Cool."[4]

It should go without saying that none of the above is the affair of the serious fiction writer, at least as far as the writing itself goes. To articulate a concern about the state of the art of fiction requires that the writer assume everyday form, either in a humanistic sense, i.e., What's Wrong With All These People?, or in a human sense, i.e., I'm Thirty-One, Working In A Mailroom, And So Far Have Earned Two Free Copies From The Shlbotnik Review. The one is good for faculty party chat and the other for commiserating with fellow writers who've just received $1.20 royalty checks from Tsouris Press. Writers can wear these concerns externally, as layers of paint, as drapery, when walking through the world in which they buy toilet paper and take the garbage out—in other words when undergoing one of the eighty-nine thousand daily tests of endurance that help to distinguish non-writing from writing—but a barrier should descend as the work begins, blocking out all concerns except those of the work and its own peculiar space and time.

---

[4]Aka "Kerouac wore khakis."

Three Axioms for Projecting a Line
(or Why It Will Continue to Be Hard to
Write a Title sans Slashes or Parentheses)

Steve Tomasula

MY FATHER WAS A machinist. Most of the fathers (and none of the mothers) who lived on our block were workers in heavy steel—a thing, as Plato would describe it, with no fuzzy lapses into that shadowland of symbols. Today, however, makers of things seem to be an endangered species. For example, everyone's probably noticed how few workers it actually takes to build a highway. Or a skyscraper. Even more revealing of the morphing of the world of our fathers and mothers into that of our own is the disappearance of "things" themselves: unlike Adam Smith's dream in which a single machine supplies pins for all the world, we liberated pin makers have not been set drifting in oceans of free time; no, we're at workstations, manipulating the symbols that everyone craves and that consequently drive our economy. In fact, the work of many jobs can be characterized as "symbolic" even if the symbols worked upon still retain some residue of Platonic "thingness": designer jeans, automobiles, perfumes, bottled water. . . . That is, the world of things has become a world of signs—a universe that both brings into being and is brought into being by symbolic codes. Perhaps it is for this reason alone that that most symbolic of all codes, the literary text, can foreshadow a future world while the contemporary world suggests the future of poetics.

In his book *The Rise of the Novel,* Ian Watt documents the interplay of text and world that produced the novel, and this genesis is a good starting point to look for the future; the line from the novel's origin through its present is fresh in terms of literary phenomenon yet old enough to provide the historical perspective necessary for a projection.

Specifically, Watt writes, the novel couldn't come into being until societal conditions made possible the autonomous individual who prospers or fails by jockeying among others in a web of social situations. What's more, the autonomous individual, especially within the middle class, had to be taken seriously enough by both writers and readers to be a subject for literature. Witness the number of novels of that era that bear the name of the main character as title: *Clarissa, Pamela, Robinson Crusoe, David Copperfield.* . . . Reflected within the pages of these and other books is a mind-set that led people to look for truth via sense perception—another contributing factor to the birth of the novel. They were grounded in a conception of time as that which unfolds rather than that which is ever-present (in Augustine's sense). These characteristics helped compose a worldview that had a historical moment and real consequences. To cite just one of Watt's examples, the institution of marriage in which the woman makes a free choice of a mate came about soonest in England and was probably a contributing factor to the rise of the novel, that eighteenth-century laboratory of romantic scenarios. That is, a culture's collective thought produces concrete consequences such as institutions like marriage, and one of these consequences in eighteenth-century England was the novel itself.

This isn't to say that these conditions caused the novel. It is more like Kenneth Burke's description of metaphor: Eskimos, he says, make certain connotations with white because of the snow-filled world in which they live. And yet we can't say that snow caused their connotations any more than we can say that a problem creates its solutions. Rather it is that the conditions allow a meaning or solution to come into existence—the solution arises out of a need to solve the problem. In the eighteenth century, Watt writes, the novel was an artistic solution to an epistemological problem: the redefinition of humans and their relationships that resulted from a belief in rationalism and an accompanying push toward empiricism. These modes of thought, and the new social orientations that accomplished them, also brought into existence literary techniques such as character portrayal through possessions (anyone could tell the type of woman Moll Flanders was from the makeup of her toilet). Or, as Burke writes, a conception of man as that being who stole fire from the gods is going to result in very different works of literature than will a conception that sees man as a link in an evolutionary chain.

Thomas Kuhn describes an analogous development in his description of paradigm shifts in science. How is it, he asks, that the Chinese were able to see dynamic phenomena like sunspots and novas that their European counterparts were blind to? Did both parties see different things when looking in the same direction? An answer can be derived partly from the history of astronomy itself. As in the evolution of literature, the techniques that arise out of the evolution of a science—the use of the telescope, for example—will surely help determine what is seen. During the Middle Ages, though, Kuhn argues, the Chinese and the Europeans saw the same things, but saw them in different relationships. Looking at the sky in a context of a static cosmology, Europeans could not "see" a comet as an astronomical phenomenon, as could Chinese who had no such restriction. And yet, Kuhn writes, these relationships or perspectives are every bit as real as their objects. For example, he continues, the critics of Copernicus who refused to believe that the earth revolved around the sun were not entirely wrong. Part of what they understood as "earth" was "fixed, unmovable position." Copernicus was calling on his contemporaries to perform the sort of gestalt-like switch our minds can make when we look at an Escher drawing and see it one moment as a flock of white birds in black space and the next moment as a flock of black birds in white space.

In the case of the novel—here taken to be an imitation of the autonomous individual within a web of social institutions—we have real changes in what is seen as well as changes in the relationships that are seen between these objects. To form an analogy with the Chinese and European astronomers, not only did the sky change around the turn of the century, but there was also a shift in the position from which writers viewed it.

That is, the absorption of Freud, Marx, Einstein, and Henry Ford brought about changes in thinking that made faith in rationalism and its accompanying social order impossible. Consequently, narrative devices such as a fixed point of view became obsolete. In their place rose technical innovations, such as those created by Henry James by which inner consciousness is portrayed; in contrast to the eighteenth-century novel, the subject of a James novel is seldom what happened. Rather, it is more often how and what someone thought they thought. In other words, in a world that is seen as relative, the modernist use of viewpoint became an instrument to explore not only a newly emerging culture but also the perspectives from which that culture was seen. The same can be said of stream of consciousness, fragmentation of the narrative, the use of irony as a master trope, and other narrative devices common to modernist novels. In fact, the alienation of the modern protagonist or the salvation of the hero through art or purity of idea can be seen as a direct outgrowth from and reaction to the bourgeois social order and novel that preceded it. So can the individuality stamped into each work—one can pick out a Hemingway novel, for example, upon hearing a single sentence. It only took time for modernism to become identified with the avant-garde: each new style was thought to be a new beginning.

After a while, though, this overturning of convention became the convention, the new orthodoxy. The tension with mainstream culture that had brought the avant-garde into existence began to lose its impetus when that same mainstream culture began to embrace it.

In the avant-garde, then, we see a high-speed enactment of one of the first axioms necessary to literary forecasting: each style or movement contains within it the seeds of its own obsolescence. This phenomenon is not confined to literature, of course. Once the drive to minimalism in painting achieved the empty canvas, painters had two options: they could begin to add elements, or they could move off the canvas, which is what some did, thereby giving the world performance art, earth art, body art, etc.

In the novel, the fact that plot lines are numerous but not infinite foretells the death of the plot-driven novel as art. And, in fact, Ortega y Gasset proclaimed the exhaustion of the picaresque novel since all of the options for plot lines had been used up. He welcomed innovations such as the turn toward subjectivity that he saw in Dostoyevsky's novels as the only way to advance the genre.

Closer to home, a break with the sort of novel Ortega y Gasset welcomed seems to be symbolized by the societal recognition of a gap between words and the objects they signify. In one of his prefaces, Henry James writes that words and stories end nowhere, but that it is the writer's job to draw a circle around them in which they will happily appear to do so. Beginning with linguists like Ferdinand de Saussure and Charles Sanders Peirce around the early part of our century and following through to deconstructionists like Jacques Derrida near the end of it, the attempt to erase the boundary that James identified can be described as nothing but an assault. We've been forced to reconsider the nature of Nature by being forced to reconsider its representation, especially its representation through language. And what many writers have concluded is that representation can in fact be of nothing. A child on a hobby horse, writes art historian E. M. Gombrich, re-presents riding without representing riding. Likewise, texts which were once thought to represent Truth or History increasingly came to be described as simulacra of representation; the words in a dictionary might seem like strata of meaning, Derrida postulates, but in fact, the definition of a word dissipates the more we try to define it. What we should be talking about instead of meaning, he argues, are "language effects." That is, if words have no single, objectively verifiable referent, then much of Western thought needs to be reconsidered. Significant for this discussion would be the reconsideration of genres such as fiction and nonfiction, which are centered on conceptions of representation.

Indeed, this reconsideration of genres points out a second axiom useful to literary forecasters: art is made according to the uses to which it is put, as can be seen by a glance at the sculptures and paintings of ancient Egypt, medieval France, Renaissance Italy, postwar Europe, or the art of any other time and place. In contemporary America, the re-patterning of knowledge is obviously dear to a number of authors and readers. And visual artists. And activists. And just plain folks. So dear that it has already eroded the kind of boundaries James took for granted as well as some that wouldn't have even occurred to him. We've witnessed especially the dissolution between traditional categories such as man/machine, history/fiction, high art/popular art, male/female, politics/image making, art/entertainment. Even something as seemingly straightforward and objective as counting heads, i.e., the census, becomes for us every ten years a battleground of semantics.

One can look at this situation and decide between the two personae available to would-be prophets: the Prophet of Doom or the Prophet of Social Improvement. Some have opted for the former, assaying the ramifications of an aesthetic that posits low culture as high (e.g., the comic book as art) and high culture as merely one of many, equally valid, stances. Prophet of Doom Hal Foster frames the debate this way: "One may support postmodernism as populist and attack modernism as elitist or, conversely, support modernism as elitist—as culture proper—and attack postmodernism as mere kitsch." Laura Knipsis, on the other hand, derives a politics of postmodernism based on both poles of feminism—the American strain that sees the past as recoverable and the Continental strain that sees the subject as text. Calling feminism the political consciousness of postmodernism, Knipsis envisions authors who are unwilling to call all the world a text—or to say that the world is nothing more than a text—and yet are able to use the tools of textual analysis to construct a critique of this text/world. Knipsis and other postmodern critics see within a recognition of noncanonical aesthetics a voice and conduit of empowerment for previously marginalized groups. This stripe of postmodern writer refuses to posit any structure, or what Jean-François Lyotard calls master narrative—such as art or myth—as the light in the chaos. Instead, the postmodern novel calls readers' attention to the operation of the literary history within the creation not only of texts but of institutions and modes of thought outside the text.

In fact, it is within Knipsis's synthesis that we see a specific instance of a third axiom: literature changes according to the dynamics of its own history as well as to the history of the world that surrounds it.

Indeed, it could be argued that a literature that ignores this double helix of art and world is not literature at all. It certainly wouldn't be "literature" in the traditional sense of an art-ful (i.e., constructed) expression of contemporary experience. As Robbe-Grillet puts it, "A Delacroix painting painted today would be grotesque." The same could be said for an epic poem—a poem about a serious subject written in a high style about a hero upon whom the fate of a people depends. Like the Delacroix painting Robbe-Grillet invents, the grotesqueness of this poem would arise from its disjunction with a world that has experienced the revolution in society and social sciences that ours has—a world in which the Japanese, for example, can change prime ministers fifteen times within a thirteen-year period without experiencing much change in their international relations. Unlike the age of *Beowulf,* the fate of a people no longer depends on single individuals. Unlike the premoderns, the state of the world no longer depends on individual families. We don't need any more Delacroix paintings, epic poems, Gothic cathedrals, baroque music, or Mies Van Der Rohe skylines because these modes of expression not only would ignore the internal history of their own art but, more seriously, would be blind to both the "things" that compose our world and the semantic relationships we now see between them. They would ignore a world that can't be called Marshall McLuhan's global village come to life but certainly can be compared to something like global village*s.*

As happened in the late eighteenth century, people today are living through a revolution in theories of knowledge, means of production, and modes of communication. A revolution in values, a breakup in power structures, and other upheavals have brought about an era distinctly different from the way life was lived before WWII. Variously called postindustrial society, multinational capitalism, consumer society, media society, and other names, our culture is today embroiled in revolutionary cultural choices, not the least of which is a reassessment of what we expect of literature. Just one societal change, the empowerment of minorities, for example, is enough to alter the nature of a nation's literature; add in the rise of the image, the fall of the Berlin Wall, and other economic, political, and epistemological changes, and the effect on how today's art is used, and therefore created, is profound. Something as ubiquitous as the Xerox machine works against the modern novel, just as the absorption of Marx, Freud, and Einstein worked against nineteenth-century realism. What we do for a living, where we live, how we live cannot be served by modern forms of expression, and writers today, as they always have during times of great social change, are in search of a new language.

Put another way, if a painting that orders space through the rigid grid of linear perspective seems anachronistic in an age of global interconnectedness and the jump cut, what are we to make of the Stephan Daedalesque art hero? or of the now antique forms of the modern novel? or of notions like purity of idea and ironic nihilism in the home of pop culture? Try to imagine Gregor Samsa enjoying a frozen yogurt at Disneyland and you'll get the idea. The reality of contemporary America is that it is no more possible to avoid pop culture than it would be to dismiss the demise of a world that could easily be divided into things and symbols, science and metaphor, material and linguistic constructions (some of which can kill).

This shift is partly the reason Linda Hutcheon claims that no serious writer today writes without attention to both plot and metaplot, fiction and metafiction. And yet this too seems to be only part of the story: the academy, reviewers, and ordinary readers take very seriously plenty of writers who seem oblivious to meta-anything. And why not? The multivocal ethos of the era demands room for modern novels as well as for nineteenth-century romances and punk sci-fi and the psychological epiphany of the realist's utterly mundane moment. That is, there seems to be a group of writers and novels that fit Hutcheon's description, the novel(ist)s of postmodern ideas; but there also seems to be another group which might be called the novel(ist)s of a postmodern climate—the works and authors that can thrive in the space created by the ideas of the first class. Thus, as Barth suggests in his "Literature of Replenishment," we have postmodern writers such as himself, Carlos Fuentes, and Toni Morrison writing alongside modernists like John Hawkes who is writing alongside premodernists like Updike—authors who write essentially nineteenth-century novels even though they are about contemporary situations and are written in contemporary language. Called domestic realism, shopping-mall realism, normal fiction, traditional fiction, or workshop fiction, these nonmodern books incorporate the techniques of modern novels but none of the modernist agenda. For example, a highly subjective point of view might be used as a probe, but the examination is likely to be performed on some bourgeois concern, not epistemology. The landscape of alienation in these books can be characterized as around-the-house-and-in-the-backyard fiction, as Don DeLillo once called it.

Considering the attention received by these nonmodern novels, we can see a second function of literature today: the novel as artifact of public speech. For example, pulp science fiction from the thirties can be read to limn the prejudices, fears, hopes, and other attitudes prevalent in the years leading up to WWII. The scholarly journals reveal other examples of this sort of pragmatic reading, especially an interest in literature as social snapshot, racial memory, or outsider documentation/artifact—an artifact that asserts "I am." Titles like "Colonial Legacies" and "The Challenge of Otherness" abound. This documentary function of literature at times flashes into the limelight when, for example, an anthology is revised and economic reality tests the theory that canon revision is merely a matter of adding chairs to the table. The addition of categories like detective fiction, comic books, science fiction, and westerns is accompanied by descriptions like "Greatly strengthened representation by women and minorities" and "commitment to expanding the American literary canon" and "extensive coverage of women, marginal, and mainstream voices." So dominant has this pragmatic function of literature become that one sees its force at such grassroots levels as the little magazines, even those produced on kitchen tables. Where once it was common for magazines that had nothing to lose to take the high road of aesthetics (the modernist religion), now it is common for the contemporary counterparts of these magazines to relegate aesthetics to political handmaiden. Where once it was common for a magazine to claim "excellence" as its only criterion, writers' guidelines are now more likely to include phrases like "looking for writers who have been excluded from publication" and "We hope to hear from writers who have been marginalized" and "especially looking for gay, minority, third world, feminist, Native American, and writers in prison." The subtext of these guidelines as well as the new historicization by the academy is that the answer to "Whose story gets told?" is at least as important as the story itself. We have called on the marginalized to perform the role of men and women of letters just as colonial America asked the same of sermon writers and nation builders.

So where will lit go from here? Will the term *Literature* fall out of use in favor of the more inclusive *narrative,* a term that can encompass the stories that will march in with new technologies as well as enable the valorization of forms already among us but shut out from serious consideration by our present vocabulary: genres of soap operas, puppet shows, talk radio, government treaties, Ice Capades, People's and/or Supreme Court rulings, the cyberpulp novel? Wouldn't this be the next step in the continuing democratization that began with the fall of feudalism? Perhaps the books that will come to stand as the most representative of our period (and therefore be the most influential to future writers) will be those that serve the two dominant functions of literature described above: those works that contribute to the redefinition of knowledge and our accompanying institutions as well as serving as "witness."

Manuel Puig's *Kiss of the Spider Woman* might be such a book. In it, Molina, a homosexual, makes up romantic stories for his cell-mate, Valentin, a hard-eyed realist imprisoned for his political activism. Molina tells his pulplike stories in the most romantic, saccharin language imaginable—a low genre transformed to art by Puig's choreography. Simultaneously, along the bottom of the page is a clinical discourse on, for example, the genetic makeup of homosexuals. The language of this discourse is objective; it uses the conventions of scientific documentation, such as the passive voice and the present tense: "As for the sexual appetite of lesbians, it is in fact stimulated, but normally remains feminine." That is, it uses language that projects authority over its subject and the juxtaposition of this scientific discourse with the languages and epistemologies of the romantic and political rebel makes us question the nature of received Truth —especially its constructed nature—all in the context of the very nonfictional world of state terrorism in Latin America.

No one can predict the future reception of this or any book, of course, or what might be written in response to it (who at Hemingway's Nobel ceremony would have dreamt that his importance would become entrenched because some scholars systematically tried to come to grips with what they saw as a despicable force?). But if we believe that (1) each movement contains its own seeds of destruction, (2) literature changes for both literary and nonliterary reasons, and (3) works will be produced according to the uses to which they are put, we can say one thing with certainty: the future novel will be different; not all things are possible in every age. Though perhaps not so different; not all things are possible in every age. Already in the brief life of postmodernism, which according to some is itself already dead, we've seen novels evolve from the form-driven OuLiPoesque to metafictional or otherwise theory-driven to the novel that takes the form and theory of the first two stages and uses them in the service of more traditional storytelling. Together these books both synthesize and scatter the history of writing by making manifest its splintered nature—and perhaps this is the very reason that the novel of the foreseeable future may not be so different from the novel of the present.

Looking at the present state of literature, we see nothing but unresolved issues, a divisible nation—which is to say the contemporary state of the novel is business as usual with the difference that in our moment we don't believe words like *history* or *reality* can be used in the singular. As the Chinese and European astronomers demonstrate, what is found is what is looked for, and our inability to step outside of our own *Weltanschauung* is precisely what makes everything appear to be going in multiple directions at once. For example, we can hope that the technologies that make niche marketing possible will free literature a bit from the demands of the two-headed god Mass Marketing/lowest common denominator, though this remains the great unrealized promise of cable TV. (One is reminded here that the problem of world starvation is one of will, not resources.) Still, zines abound. And having torn open terms like *humanities* and *art* and *science,* we've yet to become comfortable with complete open-endedness or any alternative definitions. Needless to say, we have not approached anything that might be considered universal understanding of "The Other" or even an acceptance of the fact that the linguistic construction we now caption as "The Other" requires that we never will. Given that problems like these are at the heart of the paradigm shift the novel has recently gone through, that in fact they may be its very raison d'être, it seems reasonable to expect a period of synthesis; paradigm shifts are usually as much culmination as herald. Witness the example of Newton or Einstein. Or Shakespeare or Joyce. What followed the Janus-like masterworks of these authors was a period of sustained refinement, development, testing, and acceptance or rejection of assumptions like those described above. Likewise, what will follow our moment will be a testing of the assumptions grounded in it, such as the belief that open access to publication will result in an "improved" literature. Given a conception of literature as collective memory and a political climate that includes China and Eastern Europe, a time when more does not equal better might be a long way off. But what effect will the Internet have where authors (or anyone) can pour prose into the world at the rate of 28,000 bits per second, uncensored and edited or not?

Will the Internet bring docufictional modes of narration closer to the exhaustion Ortega y Gasset identified in the picaresque novel? It really isn't hard to imagine the day when every terminally ill, sexually abused, disenfranchised person—or more ambitiously, everyone—will have had his or her fifteen minutes in print/on the screen. Or will have so seemed to readers. What happens to any genre when technology leans on the fast-forward button of its evolution? We've seen what happened to the avant-garde once it was embraced by the mainstream culture against which it had been postured. What will happen to the function of literature as that which makes the marginalized present once marginalization itself is embraced by the mainstream? Radical Rabbit Chic Redux? What will happen to the forms we've devised to crack open old hierarchies? or the will that allows the whole engine to run? "Imagination dead, imagine!" Beckett wrote. As the novel did in the eighteenth century, as it has always done, it will turn to those things that the culture it helps bring about asks of it. Which is to say, it will turn to other things. But not necessarily tomorrow. Or on command, not even GO http://www/future.lit.

SYSOUT=A

William T. Vollmann

"They," by whom I guess I mean Heidegger's *das Man,* say that the role of hard copy is declining. In MVS operating system Job Control Language, which I was once somewhat familiar with, the programmer can specify **SYSIN**, what goes into the system, what the program uses for input (a magnetic tape, for instance), and **SYSOUT**, which specifies what happens to the output. Garbage in and garbage out, they used to say. **SYSOUT=A** was a printer. When the program executed, one would get a certain thickness of green-and-white-striped fanfold computer paper covered with eccentric poems which nobody ever read from start to end. That was the sad thing. If there were a problem I might go to a certain line number and read a small way from there, then flip forward or backward until, if I were lucky, I'd figure out what had gone wrong—the worst reason to read. I used to get quite a few **ABEND S 213**s, which meant that a certain data set needed to run the program could not be found. When I did a dump of the executed program to the printer, I would look for the error message at the end, and then hopefully find a line number reference to which I could page in order to learn which data sets had abended. Then that error would be fixed, and the sheaf of paper would get thrown into the trash. Nauseating. This was why the veteran programmers did everything on screen (I forget now which **SYSOUT** that was). It was a point of pride in some quarters not to generate paper, and it should have been. I got good at that myself. Now the only time I ever print out a draft of a book or an essay is when I've finished the final draft.

In effect, my search for **ABEND**s was a precursor of those virtual reality pick-and-choose computer plots. Forget Raymond Chandler. You are the detective. Will you arrest Mr. X or Madame Y? Press a key, and the screen glares with a dozen sordid colors and makes electronic whiz-biz vomiting sounds; how excellent. "They" say that this is the future, and they might be right. Why bother to read a book from cover to cover anymore? Spot the criminal as quick as you can, and then screw the blonde babe. Go directly to bed; and collect $200 while you're at it.

Now, what would it mean to have a CD-ROM version of *Middlemarch?* You'll be Lydgate and tell him not to marry Rosamond. You'll be Bulstrode and make him come clean before Raffles shows up leering. For this to be done properly, our meta-George Eliot would have to write a whole slew of different *Middlemarch*es with hypothetical plots and twists and turns. (Let's click on Dorothea's stack.) It's possible, I grant you. If meta-George were to spend her whole life creating just this one entity, and if she were already a genius in spite of not having had time to write the other books which the original George taught herself on, then maybe it would work.

Of course a meaningful exercise would require Bulstrode, if he did come clean, to do so in a Bulstrodish way, which would mean somehow covering his tracks, which would mean not really coming clean at all, just lying in a different way. The whole point of *Middlemarch,* and of all good literature that I can think of right now, is that we are what we are. Free will is by no means an illusion, but a greater proportion of our freedom than we are willing to admit comes from random events imposed by life, which change our circumstances in such a way that reacting to them forces us to discover something about ourselves. Computer games are certainly good at presenting one with statistically bounded random events. But the big problem with computer games is that they are written by committees. One team does the graphics, another the sound. Somebody else does Bulstrode. The reason that a work of art is compelling is its unity. It is stamped all over by the imprint of one mind. A metafiction would almost certainly be a collaboration, unless meta-George is even more multitalented than we think; and a collaboration is inherently less likely to produce outstanding results, for the reason that I've mentioned.

What bothers me more about computerized books is that only people with money will be able to own them. I have seen homeless people reading paperbacks. I have never seen them with laptop computers. This doesn't mean that laptops couldn't someday become ubiquitous and disposable like the cardboard cameras which "they" now sell in drugstores, but I don't often see homeless folks with cameras, either. Or prison inmates. Or other people who might have a use for a water-swollen Signet Classic they found in some dumpster.

And this goes along with the times, that more and more the privileged people will work in their homes and shop from their homes and access the Internet and play with their computers which will make the phosphor-dot worlds more and more real as the world outside continues to go to shit. But that's irrelevant, and anyhow I don't think that the creation of great cyberart is out of the question. After all, "they" used to say that a movie could never be art. So perhaps we will have cyberdirectors and cyberwriters who will collaborate, and the special effects geeks will let us see the whole goddamned town of Middlemarch through Rosamond's eyes, and then through her husband's, but I fear that the special effects geeks will want to jazz it up to show what they can do, and then it would not be Middlemarch anymore.

Perhaps there will someday be a technology which will allow us to actually feel as Rosamond feels, to momentarily become her, and then to become somebody else feeling something about her.* And perhaps these feelings could be sculpted and shaped by masters; the art would be in creating a personality by creating the appropriate constellation of feelings, the central synchronic core (innocent, petty little vanities, say, in Rosamond's case), and then the diachronic construct of those feelings in sequence, in action. Then Rosamond would truly live. That would be art of a kind.

But complex ideas and assonances matter, too, and that is why I am loyal to my alphabet. For me the only true **SYSOUT** is **A**. And increasingly I am becoming an enemy of the phosphor-dot screen.

---

*Or, as the porn-masters would have it, somebody else simply feeling her. Such remarks continually come to my mind here because I am writing this on my computer and the process is so tactile.

Writing the Life Postmodern

Curtis White

I ONCE IMAGINED that I could attend a conference of the Associated Writing Programs without putting my writerly soul in jeopardy. I learned otherwise one brilliant Easter weekend in San Francisco, April of 1988. Heart's blood! Didn't I witness a horror then!

It was a conference-capping plenary session on THEORY! The panel consisted of a half-dozen well-meaning writers and poets (who shall go unnamed) and Alan Cheuse (who shall go named because he richly earned it). The sacrificial theorist was Henry Staten (author of *Derrida and Wittgenstein,* Nebraska, 1984). Their collective task was to make a public presentation of the facts as we knew 'em, to that point in time, about writers/poets and THEORY! How dangerous is it? What are the tolerable limits of exposure? Have spectrum analyses shed any light on artistic risk?

Among the enduring kumquats which were laid at this session, I remember as most ripe, rich, and fruitful the following:

Alan Cheuse: "What writer uses THEORY! in his fiction? No one I know of. It's irrelevant. Writers are too busy living real life, doing things like screwing each other's wives." (God knows what this leaves women writers to do. Screw their colleagues' wives, I hope.)

Emboldened by this brassy call-to-arms, the MacFlecknoes of the present, deviating no closer to sense than their august predecessor, began popping from their seats. An oily dandy with great hair like Micky Dolenz, a cravat blossoming colorfully from his entrancing poet's cleavage, and a Wildean radiance about him, said, "We can kill THEORY! We can do it! We've got the numbers! The students are in our classes! We'll organize a boycott!"

Finally, Jack Gilbert stood and announced, "THEORY! has destroyed a generation of writers and poets, and led them away from their true calling: to illuminate the human heart."

Thus the poetic soul: self-serving and macho as any literary bwana, arrogant as mice who imagine there is strength in small numbers, and poignant as candlelight cast on a shoe box in which rests a dead kitty with her favorite ball of string.

Henry Staten was admirably cool, good-natured, and self-possessed during this embarrassing reveling in the will-to-ignorance parading as the Sublime. His final communication to the assembled scribblers was delivered dead-serious, almost sternly. Pay attention, he seemed to say, for just a moment, children—"Think what you like, but the writers and poets of the present who will matter in the future will come to terms with theory."

I'm telling you, it was a courageous moment. Staten was a living repressed returned. The poetic Childe Harolds in the audience, "among but not of" the academic crowd, self-crowned with Byronic grandeur, were apoplectic with the noive of dis guy telling them that they were academics and intellectuals and therefore responsible for understanding and responding to ideas. No, man, we're angelic fluff with big balls! We're Jesus with a fifth of Jack! We're in-spired, puffed full of beeyouteeful breath!

Staten's neat trick was to demonstrate that the poetic condition in the eighties and nineties is self-loathing: I'm an academic and I hate academia; I'm an intellectual and I hate ideas.

But what did Henry "Meet Me at Delphi" Staten mean by "come to terms"? Perhaps he meant that poets need to be able to reproduce Derrida's critique of Husserl's transcendental reduction at a moment's notice on a cocktail napkin at the English department banquet. Maybe. I'd prefer to think he simply meant, "Get with it. Live in your own moment or be irrelevant."

By now everyone has received the notification:

UNTIL FURTHER NOTICE
YOU ARE IN THE
POSTMODERN CONDITION

(Address all inquiries to the appropriate French authority.)

I was giving one of my blustery, poetico-fictive-philosophico-polemical talks at Southern Methodist University last spring when a chap asked, "Define postmodernism and tell me why anyone should pay attention to it."

(Gayatri Spivak once provided me with a surefire method for responding to the hostile "questions" of antitheorists. At a reception for a visiting scholar, she waited for him to sit, then circled his chair, sari rippling, farting mordantly all the while.)

Hell, I don't know what postmodernism is. Some say it's incredulity in the face of master narratives. Some the precession of the simulacra. Some the art of the intertext. Others the cultural logic of late capitalism. Most think it's MTV or the sampling of rap. Shoot, I'm too busy fighting about it to know what it is. And that's why anyone should pay attention to it: because everybody's fighting about it. It is a culturally cathected term.

In my judgment, the archetype of the postmodern gesture is Theodor Adorno's famous epigraph to *Minima Moralia,* "life does not live." Which means that a certain form of life does not live: nineteenth-century faith in the capitalist/rationalist/instrumentalist enterprise, or faith in the death of the capitalist enterprise, or faith in a mythic—high modernist—return to a time before capital. Adorno's maxim also means that life understood as a fundamental "normative" quality of being-human no longer lives. In short, the Modern does not live, and that privileged modernist project called *humanité* does not live. Marx's "natural children" are all "complexed," hailed by a capitalist to-do they had no idea how to refuse. In Louis Althusser's terms, we are all "apparatchick."

Not happy theses, these, but theses.

Postmodern fiction, however, is not necessarily merely an expression of the postmodern condition. Postmodern fiction is also a strategic response to that condition. To be sure, postmodern fiction assumes a condition of "damage" (to borrow again from Adorno) and dutifully expresses that damage: we are text and getting textier. Language accelerates. If we used to chew words in the old days, a nutrient rich stuff that built strong bodies in at least twelve ways, it's all crank now, insidious binaries that we mainline, along with their insulting viruses. We've caught a computer's disease, every bit as weird as coming down with hoof and mouth.

Of course, there are some, like Jean Baudrillard, who would advise us that there is no option other than an ecstatic capitulation to the flow of signs. Thus the final destination of the human: a terminal. A terminal is an oxymoron: it is both a point on an open and flowing system (a computer terminal, for example) and "the end of the road," as John Barth put it. Terminus. It is the ceaseless and futile circulation that is the equivalent of stasis. (Americans have fast cars and superhighways in order to obscure the fact that they have nowhere to go that isn't already the same place.)

Unlike Baudrillard, most postmodern fiction writers continue to carry the human capacity for resentment (although they are given no credit for this by those who worry that no one is taking flashlights into the darker cavities of the human heart). Postmodern fiction is, for its most exemplary practitioners, an expression of resentment for the postmodern condition. Thus postmodernity—like every other cultural moment—is both ideology and utopia. It is self-contradictory. Better yet, it is dialectical.

The exemplary fiction writers of our moment are not countercultural gurus convinced that we can liberate Nature from the grips of the System (hippy logic); nor are they high priests to the Imagination sitting at the right hand of a divinely appointed leader (modernist strategy—pace ol' Ez); and they are certainly not the "realist" archivists of domestic drama (the curious capitalist strategy that would seek to make fiction so banal that no one, no one at all, will want it). The exemplary fiction writer of the present moment will confront postmodern problems on postmodern grounds.

I will provide three examples.

The first is John Barth's foundational essay "The Literature of Exhaustion," in which Barth argued that the "usedupness" of the conventions of classical realism and modernism can become a means of helping the "best next thing" into being. Following this essay, Barth demonstrated in his triptych novel *Chimera* how exhaustion's empty bag, when turned inside out, begins to squirm with new life. No doubt, what the bag contains is not a Christmas puppy. It is a monster, an antigeneric nasty pasted together from animal parts which to that point had not even a nodding acquaintance. *Chimera* is a novel about pushing postmodern death-in-life (there figured as artistic and personal exhaustion/impotence) until it mutates. *Chimera* is an intimation of how one outmaneuvers a failure (call it "late capitalism") which can't be otherwise defeated.

Surprisingly, Kathy Acker's application of the cultural logic of punk (henceforth C.L.O.P.) leads to conclusions and strategies similar to Barth's. Both thematically and artistically, her strategy is to use the terms of our social defeat against the defeat itself. Hence: Is our culture dead? Then I'll be deader than death. Is our culture ugly? Then I'll be uglier than ugly. Her destination, paradoxically, is new life and new beauty.

In *Empire of the Senseless,* Acker creates the "pirate" as a utopic metaphor. Pirates were the first pure laissez-faire capitalists. Acker appropriates the pirate's aura in order to go beyond the piracy of everyday life under capital. Like Donna Haraway's "cyborg" and Deleuze and Guattari's "war machine," Acker's dextrous use of the C.L.O.P. allows her the risky gambit of reappropriating the terms of our collective defeat in the name of our collective renewal.

There is little belles about Acker's lettres. But she is smart in a cultural condition determined that writers stay stupid (innocent of ideas), trivial (domestic), and therefore irrelevant (no threat to the current regime).

Finally, Mark Leyner. Leyner is, as he writes in *Et Tu, Babe,* "in a certain sense, the most significant young prose writer in America." In a certain sense, "in a certain sense" he is. For, like Dave Letterman, he is said to epitomize postmodern irony, an irony without depth and wholly without commitment. However, Leyner is to Dave Letterman as Bizarro was to Superman. He is no mere homage to Dave's World. He is its anti-Christ. The *imitatio.* The false messiah.

Leyner achieved instant "cult status" with his second book *My Cousin, My Gastroenterologist,* a work whose "instant" required months of preparatory cult marketing. They flew in the cult consultants. They did power lunch with the boys from cult R & D. Kindly, at the end of it all, Mr. Leyner was relieved of the burden of being himself. He became his own toy. Leyner Я Us. Thus relieved of the obligation of the Self, thoroughly commodified, Leyner went on to use this success/his defeat against itself. Consequently, *Et Tu, Babe* is about Team Leyner, the artist as a young multinational, the first novelist to achieve offensive nuclear capacity. Commodify me? I'll commodify myself first. Leyner's comic coup is to ironize postmodern irony. By virtue of that double negative, he is impossibly sincere.

Of course, the question remains, which Leyner is it that shows up on Letterman? Leyner the commodity, or "Leyner the commodity"? Whichever the case, it is a lesson in the capacities of the Moment to see the "significant" Leyner side-by-side with Letterman. For Leyner/Bizarro has a chunk of kryptonite implanted in his pineal gland, which is hardwired to his third eye, which mystic organ saturates "the Dave" with ultimately toxic microcuries of self-regard.

I am going to imagine, a most improbable possibility, that I have convinced North America's writers and poets that an ineluctable part of their present condition has to do with their institutionalization within universities. I do not at all mean by this that all writers are within universities (although a very large number obviously are). Nor do I mean that the most important writers and poets are within universities. In fact, the most interesting fiction coming through FC2 (the publishing organization I codirect) is from people in frighteningly impoverished and socially marginal conditions. What I do mean is that, undeniably, universities constitute one of the largest environments in which we are presently allowed to work. If writers and poets are to be responsible to the World, then a large part of that World about which we are obliged to report is, for good or bad, the university. Of course, being "institutionalized" (our madness thus confined) is never simply a good or bad thing. But even in the worst case, we need to know where we are if we mean ever to be somewhere else. If the university really were an asylum for the insane, and all the poets therein believed, as many of ours do, that they were really living in another century, in a clean, well-lighted place, with a panoramic view of *le condition humaine,* then, guess what? they are going to stay in that asylum because . . . they are crazy!

So, the best question is to ask, "Where are we now?" Objectively, really, now, in the harshest light we can find. But that "where we are," I assure you, can have nothing to do with the romantic, poetic mythologies with which we too often dope ourselves. Let us ask, then, where are we? and what is the most human, most productive, and—literally—the most *lively* posture for us to adopt within where-we-are?

Well, the idiots savants of the AWP are right to think that all is not well in the academy, but that is the case for reasons they could hardly imagine. Let me provide you with a brief (and cartoonish) history of the modern English department.

Life before Theory (or the Time of Tweed). Roughly 1930–1975. The scholar's life was predominantly male and upper-class (less so from the middle-sixties on). Scholarship was a "gentleman's calling," something someone who didn't wish to dirty his hands in commerce could do without wholly upsetting class expectations. Ideologically, the dominant was New Criticism and its modernist cult of the aesthetic. Literature as religion. There was also, significantly, the strong residual presence of historicism/ philology and its vestigial ideology of "the great books," "the classics," and "the Western tradition." As Dinesh D'Souza, Alan Bloom, and E. D. Hirsch have shown, this imperialist past is a tough little shit and never quite as dead as one would hope. Whether dominant or residual, the academy played, during the Time of Tweed, an important ideological role as the educational apparatus in which one received a proper Eurocentric indoctrination. The canon ruled supreme and unquestioned.

The Age of Theory (in which all of the above is French Fried—and to a crisp). Roughly 1975–1982. Poststructuralism and deconstruction sweep onto campus and are merged with sixties politics of various stripes, producing: Queer Theory, ACT UP, French Feminism, post-Marxism, Cultural Studies and the New Historicism. The most significant question for hiring and promotion becomes, for all camps, "Is she a theorist?" Suddenly, young faculty all avow political positions none of which are friendly to the assumptions of the Time of Tweed and especially not friendly to the canon. This is the time of Tenured Radicals, New Barbarians, etc.

Unfortunately, the brouhaha between theorists and traditionalists, splashed across the national media, spawning repeated conservative offensives from George Will, William Bennett, and Lynne Cheney, was really only a diversion from a real, and very postmodern, threat.

The Postmodern Condition (the New Regime of Performativity). Roughly 1982–present. Theory left modernity and its ideological mission not even a few shards to shore against its ruin. The postmodern moment is one of great and very rare opportunity. All is fluid. But as the molten intellectual magma cools, one particularly frightening possibility begins to take form: in the time after the end of ideology, literature has outlived its usefulness. The new word is "performance." Make your means suit our ends or else.

An instance:

At Illinois State University's 1994 English department banquet, Professor David Jolliffe of the University of Illinois—Chicago presented a talk on "workplace literacy." He argued that we were in "post-Fordist" times. People on the assembly line are no longer stampers of widgets. They are stampers of widgets who need to be able to communicate about the success of their widget stamping to the next shift. "They need literacy!" Jolliffe whispered, in a near messianic tone. And producers of hi-tech windmills are no longer watched over by foremen; rather, they organize, discipline, and assign tasks by themselves.

Thus the new usefulness of the English department (by God, at last it is useful!) is purely pragmatic. We provide the margin of literacy that allows workers the power of self-surveillance. Managers are outmoded. The proletariat no longer requires a boss. For English departments have made them self-disciplining. Foucault spoke of the fascist within; this is the foreman within.

Here is the conclusion we ought to draw from this: writers and poets, let's not fight the wrong battle at the wrong time. We look stupid defending an ideologically constructed notion of Literature that is long dead. Theory is not the enemy. It too is done. The real danger is that departments of English are to become service departments, functioning in the name of commerce. Across the board, those subdisciplines which have moved in during literature's waning hegemony (technical writing, Cultural Studies, composition/rhetoric, linguistics/TESOL) can all easily be articulated as pure service functions to the educational factory's imperative to get people ready to go to work.

Creative writing's sad responsibility in this eventuality then would be to administer the last rites of the imagination to children damaged beyond redemption on their way to the great maw of America, Inc.

So how should writers and poets respond to this situation? I think we are really in a very fortunate and important position. As artists, people for whom literature was never only ideology but also praxis, we are in a position to be able to argue that the creation and the critical study of literature should remain at the heart of what departments of English are about, not for the usual reasons of The Great Tradition, but because the study of the literature of the past and the production of the literature of the future requires two things fundamental to a human sociality: a critical awareness of where we are and how we've gotten to where we are, and the creation of our own future. This is what writers and poets have always done: engage the tradition within which they work, and then change it. Each new work of fiction or poetry is the presentation of a world within which we might choose to live.

The fault lines dividing the academic from the nonacademic, the capitalist from the anticapitalist, are not the only fractures that presently threaten the vitality of contemporary fiction. The most decisive issue concerns the rancorous split between the commercial presses and the independent presses. Since that blip on the screen which was the moment of the counterculture, when the American postmodern fiction canon—Barth, et al.—was established, the New York commercial publishing houses have, by keeping faith with their accountants only, jeopardized the meaningfulness of the literary past and the very possibility for a literary future. Marx once said that one of the principal products of capitalism was stupidity. The shit that has regularly cascaded from New York in the course of the last twenty years has performed admirably its task of keeping people stupid. What pride can be taken in a line which has given us Moral Fiction, Minimalism, the Literary Brat Pack, and now Generation X? Commercial publishing has, perhaps, not been as single-minded in this task as has television, but books have offered no one solace for, let alone an alternative to, the egregious cretinism of mass culture.

I stand with the punks: BOOKS, I too dislike them.

At least if what is meant by books is the ecological disaster one discovers at the bookstore chains. Waldens indeed. Of course, there are many important writers being published by the commercial presses: Richard Powers, William T. Vollmann, Kathy Acker, Mark Leyner, David Foster Wallace, Stephen Wright, and Paul Auster, to name a few of the better known. At present, the alternative presses have few writers of this stature. Of course, this "stature" is itself in large part a function of the commercial presses' access to the popular media. When the Fiction Collective published Mark Leyner, it could not get him on *Good Morning America;* Crown could.

Fortunately, there is much to hope from the new "underground"— Semiotext(e), RE-Search, Sun and Moon, Dalkey Archive, and FC2. It is to independent publishers of this ilk that young writers and readers, especially in urban areas, are turning in increasing numbers. What is finally significant in this situation is that now and for the foreseeable future, writers will have to negotiate this commercial/independent split in the process of creating their own artistic identity.

Yet another related writerly dilemma was recently expressed for me by Michael Silverblatt, whose KCRW radio show, *The Bookworm,* is a standard-setter in Los Angeles. Silverblatt was interviewing FC2's Ron Sukenick about Ron's new book *Doggy Bag,* recently published in FC2's Black Ice book series. Silverblatt took the following intriguing position:

(1) American literary culture is dead because there are no new readers capable of decoding books of literary complexity. Thus, it is not simply a question of who *will* read William Gaddis's new novel, but who *can.*

(2) What is most alive and authentic in book culture now speaks to the sexual and social experiences of a radically alienated youth (readers of Kathy Acker and Dennis Cooper). But this work has nothing to do with what we used to call literature.

(3) This leaves "literary" writers and readers (including Sukenick and Silverblatt) in the untenable position of having no one to speak to except those who cannot understand them. The old literary underground is too "sophisticated" to speak to blunt postpunk receptors.

I take this to be an interesting variation on the old high culture/low culture opposition. In this case, however, it is more an issue of the politics of intelligence against the politics of a very strategic "stupidity." If the only people interested in something other than commercial shit have adopted as their strategic refusal the C.L.O.P. (is the culture stupid? I'll be more stupid than stupid), what becomes of the old-style subversive politics of intellectual critique?

Silverblatt's position would seem to be that this fissure is unbridgeable. I tend to see the situation as opportune. First, the postliteracy of the C.L.O.P. is truly strategic and not nearly so "stupid" as it might seem. How else to explain the slacker fascination with theory? Outside of theorists and their graduate students, the biggest audience for Semiotext(e)-style radicalism (Baudrillard, Virilio, Negri, Lyotard, Foucault, Deleuze and Guattari) is among a young, underground intelligentsia. (They do their book shopping at Tower Records, where Semiotext(e) books are best-sellers.) In short, postpunk dissidents are not really so distant from the older culture of critique.

Second, it seems to me critically important for the older political/literary underground and the postpunk dissidents to create lines of communication. They need to speak to each other. There is something "stupid" about the intelligence of writers like Sukenick (he "doesn't get" the ideology of the Literary; he failed that course in appreciation), and there is clearly something intelligent about the stupidity of writers like Acker. What is required is a sign under which to make possible mutual (self-)recognition. Literary centers like Beyond Baroque in Los Angeles presently provide a place where those who have lost intellectual, cultural, social, and sexual moorings may meet not only as equals but as co-conspirators. During the next cultural crisis, perhaps we'll all meet at Beyond Baroque to inaugurate the next Great Refusal. For it is written that, verily, when the universities are closed for lack of funding and universal apathy, and Henry James scholars shave their heads and have them tattooed with the sign of the Tragic Muse, then will the punks pull well-thumbed copies of Hegel and Wallace Stevens from their leather vests. They'll then go, en masse, to the nearest street-side surveillance camera and sing, a capella but in a tight harmony that jars, the old spiritual from *Kora in Hell:* "Literature is damned from one end to the other. I'll do what I want when I want and it will be good if the authentic spirit of change is upon it."

I am sorry if I have, in this essay, eluded my job description: discuss the future of fiction. But for me, fiction has no future that is not first socially situated. Fiction has no timeless, innocent, or removed home. The mythology of writers in their romantic bowers, alienated from the world yet obliged to report on it, inheritors of a special suffering, ennobled by a destiny fundamentally different from that of the parasite literary critic, these myths are self-defeating. Worse, they make writers and poets irrelevant. And yet, to judge from the pages of the *AWP Chronicle* or the *Mississippi Review*'s "Workshop Issue," these myths are still very much alive.

My own diagnosis, as I have developed, would lead to these simple conclusions.

Where-we-are: institutionalized in postmodernity and threatened by the preeminent postmodern principle—pure performance, pure system.

What-to-do: BE: intelligent, critical, and creative.

I mean, by this essay, to discourage no one from her artistic projects. I mean to proscribe no one "style" over another. I do mean, assuming the garb of a Staten-like oracular seriousness, that every "Moment" has its content. We do not live in the lingering beneficence of a kindly and always "natural" sun. There is a cultural dominant, as well as a cultural vestigial and emergent. These play an often bewildering game of tag-you're-it. My point, "for the moment," for poets, writers, artists, and anyone else who aspires to something more than the status of an always-elsewhere-shuffled-subjectivity, is that we all must be sufficiently brave, serious, and daring to try "coming to terms" with, as Beckett put it, "How It Is."

Let us close with a little prayer for the death of the dictatorship of the present in the name of an always unspeakable future.

Amen.

Fernando del Paso

A Conversation with Fernando del Paso

Ilan Stavans

Dalkey Archive Press will publish Fernando del Paso's *Palinuro of Mexico* this spring. Hailed as one of Mexico's more ambitious and rewarding novels, *Palinuro,* first published in 1977, is many books at once: a political manifesto about the student massacre in Tlatelolco Square in 1968; an encyclopedic tour de force in the tradition of Cervantes, Sterne, and Perec; a medical and philosophical treatise on the mind–body dichotomy; a critical examination of Mexico's cosmopolitanism; a re-creation of life south of the border in the fifties; and, more crucially, a narrative reflection on literature and history. A devotee of American literature as well as a librarian and diplomat, del Paso parades motifs borrowed from Ambrose Bierce, James Fenimore Cooper, William Faulkner, and numerous other writers from the United States. In this respect, his monumental work is also an attempt to find communicating vessels between the cultures north and south of the Rio Grande, often perceived as diametrically opposed and abysmally unrelated. Translated into many European languages, *Palinuro of Mexico* marks del Paso's long-overdue debut for American readers.

Q: SINCE IN *Palinuro of Mexico* you function not only as the novel's author but also as a cultural commentator, I wonder if you could take a step back for a moment and assess for me its merit and achievement. Almost two decades after its original publication, what's your opinion of it? What are its excesses? Would you change anything today? Have you ever considered a revised version?

A: The novel does suffer from excess—excess in style, excess in references. The same can be said of my only other two novels: *José Trigo* (1966) and *Noticias del Imperio* (1987). But most of these excesses are deliberate. In fact, I remember once being asked during an interview why I wasn't capable of writing shorter, more condensed books. I answered that *Palinuro of Mexico* could have had some 3,000 pages and that I had made a conscious effort to abbreviate it and the result was 650 pages. By nature I'm a baroque writer, extravagant and immoderate. This is a spontaneous drive in me. At the same time, I've gone from an extremely complicated to a more accessible style. My third novel is notably less complex than the second and, similarly, the second is less difficult than the first. So I think I've made some progress—my artistic route has been from excessive complexity to relative simplicity. As for what I would or wouldn't change in the novel today, to be honest it's hard for me to say. Books are like children: once they are born, the world is theirs and they are part of the world, and our role shaping their lives diminishes as time goes by. They have their own virtues and their own paths, and the only thing one can do is witness their development and feel amazement by what they can or cannot achieve.

Q: I have with me the Mexican edition of *Palinuro of Mexico,* published in 1980. But the book first came out in Spain, by Alfaguara, in 1977—three years earlier. Why?

A: I can give you a curious explanation. The novel in manuscript was awarded the Premio Novela México, sponsored by Editorial Novaro, a publishing house, as you know, dedicated to comic strips and second- and third-rate titles. Then, Editorial Novaro established this very important prize, which was given first to the Mexican playwright and novelist Jorge Ibargüengoitia, second to the Spanish writer Juan Marsé, and in its third year to me. But a conflict arose when the owner realized that the mammoth-size brick that had earned the prize was too much and refused to publish it. But the jury didn't want to change its decision and since the owner didn't want anybody else to bring out the book, a year and a half or two went by before my literary agent, Carmen Balcells, could get it away from Editorial Novaro. Those are the vicissitudes that took it first to the Iberian peninsula and only later to Mexico.

Q: I assume the critical reaction in these two countries was very different. After all, the novel is, among other things, an investigation of the Mexican psyche, its past and present.

A: Spanish critics were a bit more generous. Both agreed, though, that the novel had an extraordinary richness, a praiseworthy poetic content, good sense of humor, but that it was an excessive book, arrogant, too ambitious, and hence, frustrating in some aspects. Its attempt to create a macrocosm was enchanting, they claimed, but it also backfired.

Q: As far as I know, the novel has been translated into French, Portuguese, German, and English. The English version by Elisabeth Plaister, of course, was first issued by Quartet in London in 1989.

A: Plaister's translation, with the exception of a tiny notice in the *Times Literary Supplement,* went totally unacknowledged in England. The reception was a disaster: nobody talked about it, I never got a single pence. The French edition came out earlier, in 1985, just as classes had resumed after the summer break, and it was a huge success. Translated by Michel Bibard, it won the prize for best foreign book of the year. Every single newspaper and literary supplement discussed and praised it. It's important to note that a good segment of its French readership, as far as I can tell, was young and enthusiastic—just as *Palinuro of Mexico* has remained an all-time favorite among the young in my own native country. In Portugal it also went unnoticed, but the German translation by Suzanne Lang (who took five years to complete it) was also successful. It was presented during the 1992 Frankfurt Book Fair and not long ago, in Munich, it won the prize for best translation. Recently, the book appeared in Holland as well, where in a few months it has sold 6,000 copies—a best-seller for such a small country.

Q: Just out of curiosity, did the Portuguese version circulate in Brazil?

A: It did, but with no reaction whatsoever. Needless to say, the Portuguese language in Brazil is quite different and thus I doubt the country is a suitable market for a dense novel translated across the Atlantic. Along similar lines, it will be interesting to see how Plaister's British translation fares with North American readers.

Q. I'm interested in your work with translators. Were any major changes made in any of these versions? Or rather, could we talk about "variations" of the book and not of "versions"? Were translators free to manipulate the text to some extent?

A: I worked with all of them by mail. Elisabeth Plaister and I corresponded for a long time, and then, almost at the end of the process, she came from Portugal to visit me for a few weeks in Paris, where I was living at the time. It's only natural that it has errors and mistakes, of course, but in my opinion it's a splendid translation.*

Q: Let me turn to the topic of polyglotism. In your career as a reader, knowledge of other languages, I assume, has been essential. You speak English and French, don't you?

A: But that's all. As a child I didn't have a bilingual education, since I went to Mexico City's public schools. My first readings of Alexander Dumas, Sir Walter Scott, Jules Verne, Eugene Sue, and Emilio Salgari were in Spanish, often in terrible translations from Barcelona and Buenos Aires. I became acquainted with Faulkner, Erskine Caldwell, and Thomas Wolfe in Spanish. My passion for a handful of dramatists also dates from these foundational years, when my spoken and reading skills in Shakespeare's and Diderot's tongues were nonexistent. Of course every so often I would come across an extraordinary translation, like the one Borges made of Faulkner's *The Wild Palms;* but these were exceptions, not the rule. I began doing some readings in French and English on my own when I turned twenty or twenty-one; but I wasn't even close to fluency. Only later, when, together with my family, I settled first in Iowa City for a couple of years, then in London for fourteen years, and finally in Paris—the whole journey a total of twenty-four years—would I master both tongues. Obviously the moment we returned to Mexico in the mid-eighties, I stopped practicing them and, as a result, I've already forgotten a lot. I could still write a letter to the dentist or an inquiry to a foreign publisher, but I certainly couldn't write literature in either of them. No, I don't consider myself an authentic polyglot. Spanish is my mother tongue—my only language.

Q: But *Palinuro of Mexico* was written after English became a tool and not an obstacle, right?

A: Yes.

Q: I ask because your Spanish seems to me bookish, foreign, its syntax alien, or at least peculiar, to native speakers. This issue of writing in one's

---

Editor's note: obvious errors have been corrected for the American edition.

own native tongue but thinking, or imagining, in another, obsesses me, and not without reason: I left Mexico in my mid-twenties, and almost right away I established a double loyalty with English. I have discussed the topic with Ariel Dorfman, Felipe Alfau, and Julián Ríos. As I think you will agree, Borges's Spanish has what I would describe as a Shakespearean— or better, a Chestertonian—twist. His grammar, the way in which he uses adjectives and adverbs, is outlandish, bizarre. Something similar can be said of Cortázar's Spanish in *Hopscotch,* also mixed with Gallicisms from his decades in France. These mannerisms, without ever losing their appeal, often become problematic: Borges's translation of Faulkner ends up turning the text into another one of his own creations. (The Argentine writer Ricardo Piglia, in his novel *Artificial Respiration,* has a section about this most curious of Borges's reversals.) All this brings me back to the Spanish of *Palinuro of Mexico.* Would it be fair to talk about a kind of "promiscuity" between Spanish, English, and French in the novel?

A: Yes, no doubt. Furthermore, while re-reading my third novel, *Noticias del Imperio,* I have discovered a tendency to imitate English syntax, a struggle between Spanish and English, and even an inclination to Anglicize and Gallicize. It comes as a natural result, needless to say, of decades in Europe. Whenever I become conscious of this metamorphosis, I try to find a neutral language, and that's why, in *Palinuro of Mexico,* almost every character (Palinuro, Walter, Fabricio, and Molkas), when using dialogue, has the same tone of voice. But I'm not really worried about this artificiality, this "pollution" between languages and styles. After all, literature is nothing but invention—sheer artifice. And perhaps I should add that beyond this linguistic "promiscuity," as you call it, Ilan, the novel is also permeated by a British sense of humor. Even though my English was poor when I arrived in London, I understood the nation's mood and state of mind rather quickly. This, I guess, comes back to one of your earlier questions: when I went over Elisabeth Plaister's translation, I realized that in English many things sounded far better, more original than in the Spanish original.

Q: This reminds me that Gabriel García Márquez once claimed that Gregory Rabassa's translation into English of *One Hundred Years of Solitude* was "more accurate" than the original, and Borges, when talking about William Beckford's *Vathek,* suggested that the original was unfaithful to the translation. These comments are fascinating, if only because García Márquez has little to do with English, but Borges, on the other hand, knew it far too well. Have you ever translated other people into Spanish?

A: Never. Or rather, never a literary text, only press releases and similar stuff. What I would love to translate is poetry, but unfortunately my knowledge of foreign languages is limited. By the way, I began my career writing sonnets, but later switched to fictional prose.

Q: Your first book, published in 1958 (at age twenty-three), is a collection of sonnets, *Sonetos de lo diario.*

A: Yes. Juan José Arreola brought it out in his series El Unicornio. And

I've written a few more throughout my life, but never more than twenty altogether. Once or twice I've experimented with free verse, but the result was very dissatisfying. The sonnet works best for me.

Q: Let's talk now about when and where you wrote *Palinuro of Mexico*.

A: In Iowa City and London. It took eight years—from 1968 to 1976, but I should add to that several more months in which I had to rectify spelling and information.

Q: How many versions did you make?

A: It depends on the chapter. For some I made many versions—twenty to thirty—and others just came out finished. An example: chapter 24, "Palinuro on the Stairs," which not long ago was published independently in book form, began as a brief description. I felt it was very theatrical and thus decided to turn it into a dramatic piece. The chapter grew as versions accumulated, until it was clear to me that there was no resemblance between the first description and the final text. Then, when the novel was finished, I burnt the manuscript. I did so because I didn't want anybody to know how I had arrived at the final product. I wanted to be the sole proprietor of a secret, which I knew I would sooner or later forget.

Q: Did the same happen with your other novels?

A: No. I have two boxes with the manuscript and notes of the first, and scattered segments of the third.

Q: The novel was written under the auspices of various grants and writing programs.

A: Early on in my career Juan Rulfo suggested that I apply to the Ford Foundation and they sent me to Iowa. I had been working as a copywriter for a publicity agency in Mexico and abandoned all that. After that I applied for a Guggenheim Fellowship, recommended by Rulfo, Miguel Angel Asturias, and Octavio Paz, who had all read *José Trigo* and were ready to support me. Thanks to the money I got from the foundation the book began to take shape. Then, in London, I began working for the BBC, where I was a newscaster and producer of programs on Latin America. And in 1985, the family moved again so that I could work for Radio France Internationale as a journalist, and finally I enlisted in Mexico's diplomatic service. *Palinuro of Mexico* obviously benefited immensely from my early globetrotting, just before the family made it to France.

Q: Tell me about the role of medicine in your novel.

A: I originally wanted to become a doctor and began medical school, but for personal reasons had to abandon it. As the book acquired its present form—and it took a long time to do so—I realized my interest in medicine was based on my passion for its romantic aspects. I began to understand that it is nothing but a science of failure. It attempts to save a person's life and, although it succeeds at times, it is truly powerless in that it cannot explain the enigmas of the human body. Our body is a microcosm and is the only thing we truly own in life: with the body we love and hate, with the body we enjoy and suffer.

Q: Julio Cortázar used the phrase "a living cadaver."

A: That's exactly what we are—a living cadaver. I'm fascinated by our endless questioning of physical limitations and by the link between body and soul.

Q: Is there any doctor that, as a writer, marked your passion for medicine? Perhaps Burton's *The Anatomy of Melancholy?*

A: I was impressed by Burton but, to be honest, there isn't a doctor–writer I admire. My attempt to establish a bridge between these two fields, literature and medical science, is self-made. Let me repeat that I'm interested in the history of medicine, but only as a romantic dream.

Q: Which isn't unlike the history of the novel as literary genre. After all, the novel's progress is also a chronology of failure, isn't it? I'm thinking of Cervantes and Diderot. . . . In its attempt to encompass the world, the encyclopedic novel, which you champion, cannot but fall short of its totalizing dream.

A: Perhaps, but my attempt in *Palinuro of Mexico* wasn't a globalizing one. I knew my limits early on, although at times, I know, it's hard to get that impression from the text. I wouldn't describe my novel as a failure, but that, of course, is up to the critics.

Q: A challenge in *Palinuro of Mexico,* or I should say an obstacle, is the constant shifting of narrative viewpoint, oscillating from the third to the first person and back.

A: I didn't set out to employ that type of literary device. It happened as the manuscript developed in the most spontaneous of ways. Suddenly, I realized I wasn't creating a cast of characters but, in fact, a single protagonist with a number of facets or masks. In that multiplicity I myself, as the novel's creator, was also included, if only because the book has a high degree of autobiographical content, even though I have mixed the autobiographical aspect of it with fiction and vice versa. The all-encompassing protagonist could at times become Cousin Walter, who ends up being another aspect of Fernando del Paso—not of what del Paso once was but of what he could have been.

Q: Perhaps that explains why Cousin Walter reminds me of Henry James's protagonist in "The Jolly Corner."

A: But this omnipresent character can also unfold into Molkas, Fabricio, and Palinuro's other friends—Molkas representing the most vulgar, unrefined aspects of this character of characters, whereas Fabricio symbolizes his most refined side. Having said that, I should say that the secondary characters—Grandfather Francisco, Mamá Clementina, Papá Eduardo, Aunt Luisa, the French botanist—are all more clearly defined and cannot be perceived as variations of the same individual.

Q: Let's then turn to the baroqueness (or neo-baroqueness) in your style, which you mentioned a while ago. When you talk about baroque prose, I cannot help but think of the differences between Mexican and Cuban literary cultures. I say this because *Palinuro of Mexico,* in spite of its multiple references to Mexican history and art, seems to me better suited alongside the works of Cortázar, Guillermo Cabrera Infante, José Lezama Lima, Severo Sarduy, Reinaldo Arenas, and Alejo Carpentier. It is self-referential, carnivalesque, parodic, and satirical, and, at the same time, it offers a variety of levels of meaning and interpretation. Of course all this has come to be known as the trademark of Cuban writers. Mexican writers, on the other hand, are much more accessible—with the exception, obviously, of Carlos Fuentes, with whom you share more than a hyperactive style. Both countries, Cuba and Mexico, inherited from the Iberian peninsula a highly convoluted, hybrid worldview, part Christian, part Muslim, part Jewish, and they added even more ingredients to the soup—in the case of Cuba a mulatto and Creole dimension, and in the case of Mexico a mestizo one. And these ingredients were in turn superseded by Oriental and Hindu influences. Our architecture is equally baroque: rococo, churrigueresque, plateresque, and other hybrid textures compete against each other for space and recognition in the very same cathedral or monastery. They turn their objects into exaggerations, or what Borges would call "caricatures of themselves." But in literature the two nations couldn't be more different.

A: Claude Roy, a French writer, once argued that pre-Columbian cultures were already baroque, meaning that in Hispanic and Portuguese America such tendencies were already in place even before the *conquistadores* stopped by.

Q: An interesting point.

A: But as you know there are, according to Eugenio d'Ors, more than twenty different kinds of baroque style. The simplest definition of baroque is a style that tries to saturate space by abusing curves to the point of hyperbole, and you will agree with me that Coatlicue, the Aztec goddess, is indeed baroque. As for my own *barroquismo,* it's influenced by Rabelais and Joyce (who, by the way, isn't exactly a baroque writer, but at the same time isn't far from one), and by more contemporary figures like Günter Grass, Lezama Lima, and Carpentier.

Q: But again, Mexican writers are somehow allergic to excess. I mentioned Carlos Fuentes as an exception, and obviously not all of Fuentes's books—certainly two or three. He was born in 1928 and you in 1935. Perhaps earlier in your career that meant you were part of different generations, but you've turned sixty and he is close to seventy, so the age difference is negligible. Fuentes has been a magnetic figure, the center of a solar system around which other writers gravitate. He has overshadowed others.

A: You're right. Today I might say we belong to the same era in Mexican literature, although, to be accurate, he began much earlier than I did, and his early novels, up until *Terra Nostra,* had an impact on me.

Q: In what way?

A: *Where the Air Is Clear* was a revelation to me. It was a novel that revolutionized Mexican fiction in that it stationed itself in a decisively urban atmosphere—its protagonist, as you know, is Mexico City. It influenced me in its attitude and openness to other styles. We were at the time reading the same set of authors: Flaubert, whose approach to the novel we admired, as well as Joyce; and in more technical terms, John Dos Passos, Hemingway, Virginia Woolf, and Faulkner. Without them we wouldn't be who we are today.

Q: More than Fuentes influencing you, I would say the two of you maintain a trans-textual, trans-temporal dialogue. He of course has been a consummate adapter, rewriting (or shall I say stealing?), say, a screenplay by Cabrera Infante, a short story by Adolfo Bioy Casares, a central motif in Henry James's "The Aspen Papers," and so on. But in your case one can talk about bridges reaching out to the other's work. In the last chapter of *Palinuro of Mexico* you mention, among many other literary and mass media names, Artemio Cruz. And in one of the early chapters your protagonist goes out to buy a copy of *Where the Air Is Clear.* Then, of course, there is the chapter "A Bullet Very Close to the Heart," in which you discuss the fate of Ambrose Bierce. In the eighties Fuentes published his novel *Old Gringo,* in which the spirit of your chapter, if not its words, are present. He even describes him as that, an "old gringo," as you had done: *viejo gringo.* Ambrose Bierce, by the way, also appears in *Noticias del Imperio.* . . .

A: Shortly after *Palinuro de Mexico* was published, I had lunch with Fuentes. At the time he told me: "Fernando, I have been told that one of your chapters deals with Bierce's experience in Mexico as he joins Pancho Villa's military forces. I don't want to read it, and I won't read it, because I'm preparing a whole novel on the very same topic, on which I've been working for a while." It's a coincidence, then, but an expected one. After all, once one writer discovers a fascinating character like Bierce, who crossed the border at age seventy-something, traveled through Mexico, and was never heard of again, the topic becomes a magnet to others.

Q: You're not only a novelist but a painter, and your pictorial art has been exhibited in various countries. Occasionally *Tristram Shandy* dares to use drawings and graphic design to express what words cannot say. Cabrera Infante paid tribute to Sterne in *Three Trapped Tigers,* where to describe darkness a full page is printed in black ink, and several graphic designs are present. Others in what I've called "the encyclopedic tradition," which includes Cortázar's *Hopscotch,* Georges Perec, Umberto Eco, John Barth, and Carlo Emilio Gadda, have also made use of this practice. It strikes me as an interesting fact that you don't, in spite of your background as a painter.

A: I was tempted, but I chose to keep these worlds separate. My view of literature is still based on its oral tradition. A good page is one that can be read and enjoyed aloud. Its sound is what really matters—one really shouldn't mess around with easy tricks.

Q: As one of its many aspects, *Palinuro of Mexico* can also be approached as a political novel. One of its leitmotifs is the student massacre, in October 1968, at Tlatelolco Square. Just as the Olympic games were about to begin, the Mexican government, as you well know, was facing heavy pressure from social forces asking for democratic change. But refusing to open up, the ruling party under the leadership of President Gustavo Díaz Ordaz ordered the army to confront the student uprising with tanks and bullets. Many thousands died, and many more were injured. Of course the Tlatelolco incident appears numerous places in Mexican literature, from Elena Poniatowska's memorable *Massacre in Mexico* to books by José Agustín, Gustavo Sainz, and Parménides García Saldaña. But your work has a special place on that shelf: the protagonist in *José Trigo* is killed by army squads at Tlatelolco; and Palinuro dies too, although at home, after being badly beaten in the *zócalo*—or perhaps, he begins a new life, in Tlatelolco. And yet, by 1968 you were thirty-three, too old to be an undergraduate at the Universidad Nacional Autónoma de México or the Instituto Politécnico Nacional, the two academic institutions where the uprising began. Thus, *Palinuro of Mexico* is, in a sense, about political nostalgia.

A: You're right. By 1968, still in Mexico, I had already begun writing the novel (under another title). I was married and had a petite bourgeois life. I witnessed the student uprising, but was never a participant. I've always been a left-wing intellectual, although a more moderate one in recent years. I was active during the Bay of Pigs protests, against the United States. And yet, the Tlatelolco incident left a deep mark on me. Suddenly I had a new character, named Palinuro, a medical student killed in 1968, and I wanted to make use of him. Of course by then I had already read Cyril Connolly's *The Unquiet Grave* [published under the pseudonym of Palinurus], which I had received as a gift from a poet friend, Francisco Cervantes. This new character forced me to return to the Mexico City of the fifties for the novel's setting, which—it remains a curious fact to me—didn't bother any Mexican readers. The novel had begun as a re-creation of my adolescent years, particularly of my high school years in Justo Sierra Street. Then I realized that Palinuro needed to die in 1968, but since I didn't want to sacrifice what I had already written, I let the discrepancy in dates stand. The Justo Sierra milieu attracted me enormously, and I regretted abandoning it for a sterile atmosphere like the Ciudad Universitaria campus. But Palinuro had imposed himself as the novel's heart and there was nothing I could do. And since my protagonist in *José Trigo* had died at Tlatelolco, I felt terrible about repeating myself. So I decided Palinuro would be beaten in 1968, and only afterwards he would die. This has created confusion among readers: critics and careful readers have misinterpreted my words, claiming Palinuro was indeed another victim during the massacre.

Q: Your reply brings up a crucial issue: the tie, no doubt problematic, between the Mexican government and the country's intelligentsia. I wouldn't want to repeat myself either, nor to devote too much time to a topic that has soaked up incredible amounts of ink. Latin American writers and artists, as you know, often begin their careers as opponents of the government, speakers for the masses, antagonists of the powers that be. But sooner or later, they end up embracing the very enemy they vilified and fought in their younger days. The examples are numerous, including Octavio Paz and Carlos Fuentes. Could we also include you on the same list? After all, since the mid-eighties you've been part of Mexico's diplomatic service. And now you direct the Biblioteca Iberoamericana "Octavio Paz" in Guadalajara, funded by the government. Have you betrayed your adolescent principles? Should we, readers of today, read *Palinuro of Mexico* from a different perspective, and not, as has been done, as a form of protest?

A: It's easy, at least in Mexico, to talk about "the government," "the state," as if they were nothing but abstract entities. One has friends in the government, longtime friends. Besides, very valuable writers and artists, from José Vasconcelos to Jaime Torres Bodet, have worked for Mexico's government since . . . well, since time immemorial. Don't forget that our economy is shaped in such a way that the thinking person, once a commitment to art or literature is made, has very limited options in order to earn a living. In my case, I'm far from earning enough money from royalties, prizes, and awards to support my family. Mine has been what I would call a *succès d'estime*. Also, after years in London and Paris, my decision to enter the diplomatic service became a kind of return—a return to my homeland, a return to my soul and sources. It allowed me to return to the study of Mexican pictorial art, music, and dance, and to help disseminate them. Which means that I have a clear conscience, to the extent that I represent the country's politics from a cultural perspective, not the country's politics from the political side.

Q: Finally, I have been thinking about your job as a librarian, which, in many ways, is what you do at Biblioteca Iberoamericana. Hispanic American civilization has a long tradition of literary figures becoming heads of major libraries, from our archetypal one, Borges, to Leopoldo Lugones, Alfonso Reyes, Paul Grousac, and so on. Add to this the fact that another aspect of *Palinuro of Mexico* is its cataloging of books from Hispanic, Anglo-Saxon, and French cultures. What about your personal relationship with books?

A: To be honest, my duties as director of Biblioteca Iberoamericana— which is very small, 18,000 titles, created only in 1991—leave me little time to have one. And yet, my relationship with the book is quite close. Before opening one, I always begin by smelling a book. Old books of course smell better. In recent ones, the smell is neither pleasant nor very distinct. Before leaving Mexico for England, I had some two thousand volumes of my own, which I had to store for more than two decades. I love old-fashioned hardcovers. But I've ceased to read. I don't really keep up with recent publications. Instead, I devote my time to the art of re-reading. Lately I've been re-reading Joyce, *Don Quixote,* and the Bible, which continue to amaze me for their inexhaustible nature.

On Returning from Chiapas:
A Revery in Many Voices

Rikki Ducornet

1. The One Pearl

> In this country everyone dreams. Now the time has come to
> awaken . . .
>
> —Subcomandante Marcos, "Two Winds:
> A Storm and a Prophecy" (*VF* 33)

IRANIAN GNOSTICISM offers an exemplary text called *The Hymn of the Pearl*.
It proposes the mystical itinerary of a king's son who, like Christ, makes his
way down into the world in order to recover the One Pearl from the depths
of the sea. The sea is in fact our world submerged in a drunken sleep, and
the One Pearl represents the soul. It is guarded by a serpent—not the serpent that offered gnosis to Adam and Eve, but chaos: that venomous principle.

The searcher's itinerary takes him first to Babel—there where the mud-
dling of tongues confounds the cause of brotherhood—and then to Egypt,
the land of black earth and alchemy. There he is made to drink the wine of
sleeping and forgetting. He comes to resemble his captors; without a quest
he is a slave. But then a letter from "home" arrives—a summons to awakening. It is a call to being, the Gnostical calling forth of the sleeper's innate
capacity for becoming. Not surprisingly, the words of the letter mirror the
words that are written on the seeker's heart. They rouse him from his slumber and illumine his path. Empowered, he charms the serpent and claims
what is his.

To continue a moment longer with Gnostical metaphors, recall how
Kafka's Barnabas—*the only messenger sent to K*—is himself the message.
The message, the wakening call, is love, love in what may be its most self-
less form: brotherhood. If what is written on the pearl seeker's heart is his
own innate capacity for moral being and his only chance for transcendence,
Barnabas is K's only chance for being truly human. This is why *The Castle*
is such a tragic book. K is blind, incapable of reading into his own heart,
incapable of seeing that Barnabas is his brother.

Kafka's vision of a corrupt, frenzied, and unjust world was precipitated
and informed by his own father's extensive holdings and brutal treatment of

those in his service. (He once threatened to bone his son like a fish.) In fact, the Kafka microcosm very neatly mirrors industrialized Czechoslovakia. A self-congratulatory, self-perpetrating patriarchy, racist, classist, and burdened with acute social, economic, and political contradictions, Kafka's Czechoslovakia is emblematic of a modern and universal predicament.

Which brings us to Mexico. Exemplary castle of the Third World in crisis, it is here, at the end of this most tragic of centuries, that a voice resonates like a call to being: "When the storm subsides, when the fire and rain leave the earth in peace once again, the world will no longer be the world but something better" (Subcomandante Marcos, *VF* 33). And it is here that a grass roots revolution is taking place of international significance: "The uprising coincided with the enactment of the North American Free Trade Agreement. The Zapatista army called NAFTA a 'death sentence for Indians,' a gift for the rich that will deepen the divide between narrowly concentrated wealth and mass misery, destroying what remains of their indigenous society" (Noam Chomsky, *FW* 176). "We were going to enter into NAFTA like Christ with all his beggars and sit happily at the banquet; or was the United States contemplating the inclusion of the indigenous people into the trade agreements? There are more than 6.4 million Indians in our country" (Elena Poniatowska, *FW* 104).

Fostered in the name of national unity and national pride, and founded on tribal prejudice and the law of exclusion, NAFTA brings nothing so much to mind as Kafka's take on Babel, the Great Wall of China, that dogma full of holes. The extreme alienation of the Mexican people, half of whom live below subsistence level, is shared by the dispossessed all over the planet—dispossessed of historical context, of cultural integrity, of a past, a future, of dignity, of landscape: "[They] saw forests being cut down to become supports for the wall, saw mountains being hewn into stones for the wall" (Kafka, *CS* 237). However, the struggle goes back to the time of the conquest: "The machine that Christopher Columbus hammered into shape . . . was a kind of . . . medieval vacuum cleaner. The flow of nature . . . was interrupted by the suction of an iron mouth, taken thence through a trans-atlantic tube to be deposited and redistributed in Spain" (Antonio Benítez-Rojo, *RI* 6).

Listen to the testimony of one of the New World's rare travelers who had the courage to remain wide awake:

The pearl fishers dive into the sea at a depth of five fathoms, and do this from sunrise to sunset, and remain for many minutes without breathing, tearing the oysters out of their rocky beds where the pearls are formed. They come to the surface with a netted bag of these oysters where a Spanish torturer is waiting in a canoe or skiff, and if the pearl diver shows signs of wanting to rest, he is showered with blows, his hair is pulled and he is thrown back into the water, obliged to continue. . . . At night the pearl divers are chained so they cannot escape. —Bartolomé de Las Casas (*DI* 99-100)

... they go towards
a sea without its dawns
those who hide their hunched backs
those who hide burns under shawls
those who weep when they hear music
those who weep when drinking water
—Ambar Past (*SS* 2)

2. These Things Happen

I don't know
in the mountains
these things happen
—Mónica Mansour (*MM* 33)

Beyond a certain point there is no return. This point has to be reached.
—Kafka (*BON* 87)

I have recently, with three friends (Anne Waldman Andrew Schelling, and Jonathan Cohen), returned from San Cristóbal de las Casas, there where Bartolomé de Las Casas was, briefly, bishop. The present bishop, Samuel Ruíz García, has a profound and engaged respect for the people of his diocese, the dispossessed Maya of Chiapas: "We have to be on the side of those who are suffering the most," he told an interviewer. "We found ourselves needing to build an authentic church" (*FW* 72). Just like those who have taken up arms in order to live, Bishop Ruíz is a "professional of hope." In a political context in which people are reduced to slaves and land to raw materials for industrial exploitation, in which laws are determined by markets and not by the demands of justice, and markets by profits and not by the essential needs of the people, the idea of brotherhood is a subversive idea. As does Barnabas in the land of the Castle, Bishop Ruíz threatens the oppressive system in place, an economic system of such violence that, as Subcomandante Marcos describes it, "one and a half million people have no medical services at their disposal . . . 54 percent of the Chiapan population suffers from malnutrition. . . . Education? The worst in the country . . . of every one hundred children, seventy-two do not finish first grade" (*VF* 21). Says Ruíz: "It should be fully understood that the Kingdom of God is not constructed in eternity, although it ends there, but that it is built here, starting with the poor, that is what Jesus preached" (*FW* 72).

The paradox at the heart of Christianity is palpable in Chiapas where the Catholic Church—historically the prime oppressor—is represented by a bishop whose teachings include the Mayan Book of Creation—

Pain! That's all you've done for us. Our mouths are sooty, our faces are sooty. By setting us on fire all the time you burn us.
>
> —the cooking pots speak in the *Popol Vuh*

—and a bishop who knows the fight for human dignity is not only spiritual and existential, but economic and political. In Ruíz's hands the church has become (and for this he is risking his life) an animating and a liberating force. "I care little for theology," says Ruíz; "what's important is liberation" (*FW* 72), words that bring to mind the great *campesino* revolutionary Emiliano Zapata, who proposed that tyranny is overthrown not on the battlefield alone but by "hurling ideas of redemption."

> Everything is red, I tremble. The phantoms of fright, of
> the great fear, boil in my mouth.
> —David Huerta, from "Incurable" (*LW* 137)

In 1992, what remained of the communal lands from the land reforms of the 1930s under Cárdenas were converted into salable properties to facilitate Mexico's entry into NAFTA. Many farmers were forced to sell the land that sustained them.

> Here you are dispossessed
> and belong to the nothing of nobody
> —Kyra Galván, from "City Woman" (*MM* 65)

The Maya have pushed deeper into the forests in order to plant their crops of corn, beans, and coffee. On the road to San Cristóbal we saw corn growing along the steep flanks of the mountain among rocks. Some trees left standing are trimmed of branches taken for firewood. The eroded soil reddens the roads to San Andrés Larrainzar, to Zinecantán, San Juan Chamula, Chenalhó. This claiming of forest is born of necessity; the Men and Women of Corn—the Tzeltales, Tzotziles, Ch'oles, Tojolabales, Zoques, Mames, Zapotecos, and Lacandóns—are starving, their children so weakened they die of whooping cough and measles. The poet Ambar Past,* who publishes *La Jicara*—one of the world's loveliest literary journals—in San Cristóbal, told us: "The winter I arrived here, all the children of the nearby village of Magdalenas died. *All the children died.*"

> The dead come to us when we're dreaming (Past, *SS* 21)

---

*Ambar Past is currently translating contemporary Mayan poetry into Spanish and English. This work will be the focus of a future essay.

1984: Mexico City
The Resurrection of the Living

The Mexicans make a custom of eating death, a sugar or chocolate skeleton dripping with colored caramel. In addition to eating it, they sing it, dance it, drink it, and sleep it. Sometimes, to mock power and money, the people dress death in a monocle and frock coat, epaulettes and medals, but they prefer it stripped naked, racy, a bit drunk, their companion on festive outings.

Day of the Living, this Day of the Dead should be called, although on reflection it's all the same, because whatever comes goes and whatever goes comes, and in the last analysis the beginning of what begins is always the end of what ends.

"My grandfather is so tiny because he was born after me," says a child who knows what he is talking about.

—Eduardo Galeano (*CW* 275)

In Mexico, poetry and revolution join hands, and Bishop Ruíz is only one messenger in a land that crackles with signification. Says Elsa Cross, a poet who is also a philosopher of religion: "Poetry is the foundation of the self through the world . . . a constant perception, an inner sound, a way of loving life" (*MM* 139). Writes David Huerta: "Now, writing is a form of the body" (from "Incurable," *LW* 137).

3. Let's Suppose

Let's suppose a zone of the world falls together
from Atlantic to Pacific,
from Portugal to Japan;
from the Mediterranean to the North Sea
to the eastern Arctic.
Let's suppose strange myths lift
from the ancient caves of Altamira
and the ruins of Turkistan,
something like Viking ships
and fresh legends of Tartars and samurai.
Let's suppose the Yankee government doesn't please them
and they decide to destabilize it.
—Elena Milán, "Hallucination I" (*MM* 87)

In the early evenings of winter, the city of San Cristóbal mists over; we were there late summer and each afternoon watched the rain clouds gather, the weather forming. The streets, many paved with stone, some of earth, are deep; we easily imagined those streets filled with rushing water during the season of rain. And we imagined the streets—streets in which Tzeltal, Tzotzil, Ch'ol, Tojolabal, Zoque, and Lacandón are spoken—filled with Comandante Ana María's freedom-fighters come down from the mountains to declare war: "Today we say Basta ya!"

"To our surprise, we found out there were Indian women among the leaders of the EZLN in the Lacandón jungle. Women who led battalions and gave orders in a clear, unflinching voice, women called Ramona, Petra, Ana María, Jesusa, Chabela, Amalia. Women who did not know how to read and write and who did not Speak Spanish. . . . All of them looked like Rigoberta Menchú, except for the fact that they did not wear beautifully embroidered blouses and sashes, nor did they knit ribbons into their thick black braids, but carried two bandoliers of cartridges over their shoulders and a gun strapped onto their hips. These women were hidden away in the muddy trenches in a mountain pass, or behind a red bandanna. Anonymous women were leading an army of two thousand Zapatistas"(Elena Poniatowska, *FW* 104-5). The resurgent capacity of the collective memory of the Maya was now tested and proven: despite five hundred years of systematic violence, it served as a force for liberation and a source of self-determinism. Writes Elaine Katzenburger: "Public sympathy for the Zapatistas was immediate and overwhelming. Demonstrators filled plazas throughout the country— and in many foreign cities as well—holding banners that read, 'We are all Chiapanecos.' It soon became apparent that the government would be forced to acquiesce to the growing international demand for a cease-fire. A sense of shared triumph began to spread. On the day that the official cease-fire was declared, there was a large demonstration in Mexico City. Over 100,000 people marched together shouting 'First World, HA HA HA!'" (*FW* ii). It was as though K had dared storm the Castle and rudely rouse Herr Klamm from his slumber. "We do not receive any help from foreign governments, persons or organizations. We have nothing to do with narco-trafficking or national or international terrorism. We are tired of years of abuse, lies and death. We have the right to fight for our lives and dignity. We have at all times obeyed international laws in war respecting the civil population" (Subcomandante Marcos, in "A Message to North America," *VF* 17).

Marcos does not see himself as the leader of the Maya, but in their service, and in the service of a great idea: the idea of dignity. In other words, Marcos is not interested in ideology in the same way Ruíz is not interested in theology. In this unique revolution, ideology and theology have been usurped by a passion for liberty. Which makes for the most *poetical* of revolutions—one that André Breton would surely have applauded for its "convulsive beauty." In his justly famous "Two Winds: A Storm and a Prophecy" (August 1992, published in *La Jornada* 27 January 1994), Marcos manages not only to give a concise map of the crushing exploitation of Chiapas, but to offer a vision of renewal. More than a response to tyranny, more than a list of grievances, more than a demand that essential needs be met, and swiftly, "Two Winds" is a summons, a message of urgency rising from a dying world, a wakening call: "This wind will blow from the mountains born under the trees and conspiring for the new world, so new that it is scarcely an intuition in the collective heart it animates" (*VF* 25).

The world tells me what has to be. There is a living flame.
I shall have to say what I must say—or be silent.
　　　　　—David Huerta, from "Incurable" (*LW* 139)

Repeated to the end of centuries
it vibrates in the ear of stone . . .
　　—Elsa Cross, from "Canto Malabar" (*MM* 147)

Before ending, I wish to return, briefly, to Kafka, whose fictions illumine an inevitability: hatred or indifference of the Other (and indifference is just one of hatred's many faces) leads to a sickness of the heart. Among the many examples Kafka offers is the figure of Pallas in the fable "A Fratricide." From his balcony, Pallas silently observes a murder; he does nothing to stop it, although a cry from him would suffice. Once the corpse lies bleeding in the street, Pallas is filled with self-loathing and "chokes on the poison in his body" (*CS* 402). Else the world be the black mirror of Kafka's darkest premonitions, let us look to Mexico, and let us listen:

A wind rises up and everything is resolved. He rises up and walks to meet with others. Something tells him that his desire is the desire of many and he goes to find them. —Subcomandante Marcos, from "Two Winds" (*VF* 33)

What, then? My feet call to me with a deep tenderness, a
　　　pair of neutral feet, terrestrial; feet of a human being,
　　　pieces of single and doubled flesh, feet of deep and
　　　hopeful walks.
　　　　　—David Huerta, from "November Rain" (*LW* 137)

ABBREVIATIONS FOR WORKS CITED

BON: Franz Kafka. *Blue Octavo Notebooks.* Trans. Ernst Kaiser and Eithne Wilkins. Cambridge: Exact Change, 1991.

CS: Franz Kafka. *The Complete Short Stories.* Trans. Willa and Edwin Muir. New York: Schocken, 1971.

CW: Eduardo Galeano. *Century of the Wind: Memory of Fire III.* Trans. Cedric Belfrage. New York: Pantheon, 1988.

DI: Bartolomé de Las Casas. *The Devastation of the Indies.* Trans. Herma Briffault. Baltimore: Johns Hopkins Univ. Press, 1992.

FW: Elaine Katzenburger, ed. *First World, HA HA HA!* San Francisco: City Lights, 1995.

LW: Juvenal Acosta, ed. *Light from a Nearby Window: Contemporary Mexican Poetry.* Trans. LaVonne Poteet and Nancy Joyce Peters. San Francisco: City Lights, 1993.

MM: Forrest Gander, ed. *Mouth to Mouth: Poems by Twelve Contemporary Mexican Women.* Trans. Zoe Anglesey, W. S. Merwin, Forrest Gander, Jenny Goodman, and Ofelia Ferran. Minneapolis: Milkweed, 1993.

PV: Popol Vuh. Trans. Dennis Tedlock. New York: Simon & Schuster/Touchstone, 1985.

RI: Antonio Benítez-Rojo. *The Repeating Island.* Trans. James Maraniss. Durham: Duke Univ. Press, 1992.

SS: Ambar Past. *The Sea on Its Side.* Trans. Jack Hirschman. Sausalito: Post-Apollo, 1994.

VF: Ben Clarke and Clifton Ross, eds. *Voice of Fire: Communiqués and Interviews from the Zapatista National Liberation Army.* Trans. Clifton Ross. Berkeley: New Earth, 1994.

Contributors

SVEN BIRKERTS is the author of *The Gutenberg Elegies: The Fate of Reading in an Electronic Age, American Energies: Essays on Fiction,* and *An American Wilderness: Essays on Twentieth-Century Literature.* He teaches at Harvard University and reviews books for a variety of publications.

MELVIN JULES BUKIET's most recent book is *While the Messiah Tarries* (Harcourt, Brace). He has published in *Antaeus* and *Paris Review,* and is the fiction editor of *Tikkun.* He teaches at Sara Lawrence College.

MARY CAPONEGRO is the author of *The Star Café* (Norton) and has just completed a second collection of short fiction. She teaches at Hobart and William Smith Colleges in upstate New York.

PETER DIMOCK is a senior editor at Vintage Books and Director of Academic Marketing for Random House.

RIKKI DUCORNET recently published her fifth novel, *Phosphor in Dreamland* (Dalkey Archive). She is also the author of *The Complete Butcher's Tales* and is currently writing a second collection of tales. She teaches at the University of Denver.

JONATHAN FRANZEN is the author of two novels: *The Twenty-Seventh City* and *Strong Motion.* He lives in Manhattan.

JANICE GALLOWAY is the author of one book of short stories, *Blood* (Random House), and two novels: *The Trick Is to Keep Breathing* and *Foreign Parts* (both Dalkey Archive). She lives in Glasgow.

GERALD HOWARD is an editor at W. W. Norton. His essay will appear in *The Millennial Muse,* a forthcoming collection edited by Sven Birkerts.

CAROLE MASO's four novels were released in paperback last year: *Ghost Dance, The Art Lover* (both Ecco), *AVA* (Dalkey Archive), and *The American Woman in the Chinese Hat* (Dutton). Last fall she became the director of the creative writing program at Brown University.

BRADFORD MORROW is the editor of *Conjunctions* and the author of three novels: *Come Sunday, The Almanac Branch,* and (most recently) *Trinity Fields.* He lives in New York City.

CHRISTOPHER SORRENTINO's first novel, *Sound on Sound,* was published last year by Dalkey Archive. He lives in San Francisco.

ILAN STAVANS, a novelist and critic, teaches at Amherst College. His most recent books are *Bandido* (HaperCollins) and *The One-Handed Pianist and Other Stories* (Univ. of New Mexico Press). He is currently editing *The Oxford Book of Latin American Essays.*

STEVE TOMASULA is the fiction editor of *Private Arts.* He teaches at the School of the Art Institute of Chicago, and lives in South Bend, Indiana.

WILLIAM T. VOLLMANN is the author of numerous books of fiction and nonfiction. His next book, *The Atlas,* is due out from Viking this spring. When not traveling he lives in Sacramento, California.

DAVID FOSTER WALLACE is the author of the novel *The Broom of the System* (Penguin), the short story collection *Girl with Curious Hair* (Norton), and the novel *Infinite Jest,* recently published by Little, Brown. He teaches creative writing at Illinois State University.

CURTIS WHITE is the author of four books of fiction: *Metaphysics in the Midwest, The Idea of Home* (both Sun & Moon), *Heretical Songs,* and (most recently) *Anarcho-Hindu* (both Fiction Collective). He co-directs Fiction Collective 2 and teaches at Illinois State University.